WORLDS ENOUGH

Worlds Enough

THE INVENTION OF
REALISM IN THE
VICTORIAN NOVEL

Elaine Freedgood

PRINCETON UNIVERSITY PRESS
PRINCETON & OXFORD

Published by Princeton University Press
41 William Street, Princeton, New Jersey 08540
6 Oxford Street, Woodstock, Oxfordshire OX20 1TR

press.princeton.edu

Library of Congress Control Number 2019934907
ISBN 978-0-691-19330-4

British Library Cataloging-in-Publication Data is available

Editorial: Anne Savarese and Jenny Tan
Production Editorial: Jill Harris
Jacket Design: Chris Ferrante
Production: Merli Guerra
Publicity: Alyssa Sanford and Keira Andrews
Copyeditor: Hank Southgate

Jacket image: Twelve-inch terrestrial globe gores. Rand McNally, 1887 /
Library of Congress Geography and Map Division, Washington, D.C.

This book has been composed in Miller

Printed on acid-free paper. ∞

Printed in the United States of America

10 9 8 7 6 5 4 3 2 1

For Debra, my next of kin.

CONTENTS

Worlds Enough

THERE ARE MANY Victorian novels that circulate in the academic and popular imaginations, and they have changed radically over the past 150 or so years. One is integrated, coherent, and conservative. It keeps people in place: in their countries, colonies, kitchens, and castles. Its time is empty and homogenous. It has been the fall guy and the straw man for the formal intricacies of the eighteenth-century, modernist, and postmodernist novels: it is before and after the nineteenth century that innovation happens, in which the uninterrupted diegesis formed by the Victorian omniscient narrator and the narrated world are examined, disrupted, and discussed in the novel itself, creating layers and layers of narrative and nuance.

This state of affairs has also meant that other novels—Irish novels, Nigerian novels, lesbian novels, Dalit novels, and other aspirational fictions—are in the waiting room of literary history. Their formal ruptures are accidental and messy and the result of underdeveloped literary sensibilities, especially when it comes to "form." Realism is the ur-form of the novel: the point of arrival and departure, the apex of representation that is also an endpoint, and a dead end. It is anomalous and powerful; its aspiration to reference is unique in literary history, a magnificent achievement that quickly becomes an embarrassment, even, as George Levine puts it, what seems like "an historically inevitable mistake."[1]

---

1. George Levine, *The Realistic Imagination: English Fiction from Frankenstein to Lady Chatterley* (Chicago: University of Chicago Press, 1983), 1.

Worlds Enough suggests how we might unthink novel history and restore the full oddness of the nineteenth-century novel, putting aside "classical realism" in favor of a novel full of self-reflexivity and formal hijinks. We might find narrative modes that ask readers to live in geographies that are fictionally and geopolitically "realistic" (mapped in various fictional ways) and "real" (findable on an actual map) but otherwise not humanly imaginable or phenomenologically available. Indeed, this was the Victorian version of the nineteenth-century novel in the eyes of many of its critics from the 1850s to the 1960s. It is not until the 1970s and '80s that the idea of the Victorian novel as a theoretically realist novel emerges, and with it, a set of stipulations that earlier critics had never found in that novel, and not because they had no theory. A key feature of literary criticism is that we regularly forget it. And Victorian literary criticism has been particularly forgettable. Yet its tenets, which were heavily Aristotelian and dramatic, held their own for more than a century in Anglo-American novel criticism.

I am not trying in this book to tell the true story of the form of the Victorian novel, or the criticism of that form. Indeed, my story is selective and full of gaps and omissions. In trying to restore the Victorian novel's formal problems and its lack of formal coherence, I am looking at two kinds of critics: those who appreciated these problems and those who have smoothed them over. This means that many mainstream figures in Victorian novel studies and novel theory more broadly may be omitted from my account. I am encouraging the idea of "setting aside" definitive stories in favor of provisional critical assemblages that might allow us to remember some forgotten ideas, and to revise the current status and stature of the Victorian novel. I am suggesting that we take the Victorian novel as an object of study that we have imagined intensely in varying ways from decade to decade. It is this imagining that is the most important activity: genre is historically contingent, as Michael McKeon and others have argued, and so is its criticism.[2]

The Victorian novel is annexed to a larger nineteenth-century "realism" as structuralism and poststructuralism are translated into English. It attains a certain (imagined) stability of its representational world, a noninterfering paratextual apparatus, denotation that functions as *both* reality effect and a referential scaffolding that manages to be consistent with fictionality, as well as omniscient narration, theorized variously, but preserved as the hallmark of the nineteenth-century novel. *Worlds Enough* takes up each of these features of realism in various nineteenth-century fictions, asking if we already think of them as essential—and ubiquitous—components of that fiction, and then continually "find" or identify those features in the novels that critics have perhaps helped us to homogenize into a recognizable realism through the construction of Victorian "forms." And these forms, Roland Barthes writes, "become autonomous objects, meant to signify a property which is collective and protected, and this object is a trouble-saving device."[3] Eventually, though, these forms make trouble, as we forget that we made them and their autonomy comes to guarantee our own autonomy as critics. That is, if we invoke form, we are understood as truly knowing, in some guild-like fashion, the works we discuss.

But the Victorian novel was not always imagined as formally coherent or as realistic in a good way: its lack of unity, the intrusive omniscient author, and multiple plots militated against any positive sense of this term. Indeed, the Victorian novel has seen a striking lack of critical consensus or continuity. Between the 1850s and the 1960s, these novels were sometimes praised for their ability to bring certain social truths to fictional life, but just

2. George Levine, *The Realistic Imagination: English Fiction from Frankenstein to Lady Chatterley* (Chicago: University of Chicago Press, 1983), 1.

3. Roland Barthes, *Writing Degree Zero*, trans. Annette Lavers and Colin Smith (New York: Hill and Wang, 2012), 27.

as often pilloried by critics for their formal failures. Victorian novels were compared unfavorably to their French and German counterparts (which were understood to be shorter and better), and they were often regarded as realistic in a bad way: relentlessly transcriptive of trivia.

In a series of theoretical upgrades and transnational mergers, beginning in the 1970s and gaining major steam in the 1980s, the nineteenth-century British novel was reimagined as realistic (in a French way), reactionary, and great. Realism, in novel history of the same period, became the point of representational plenitude to which early novels aspire and the point of representational exhaustion from which modernist and postmodernist novels flee.[4] *Worlds Enough* revisits some of this critical history, which is typically forgetful of itself, and restores the formal messiness of the Victorian novel before its structuralist and poststructuralist rehabilitation. This rehabilitation is, paradoxically, not celebratory. It provides for ideological unmasking: narration becomes powerful because it is constructed as a ruse of power.

This book seeks to find out how a literary-historical undoing can liberate the now-normative nineteenth-century British novel from its heavy centrality in Anglophone novel history and explore what we can read if we read against the grain of our entrenched sense of its "realism" and formal coherence. Once we unhitch the Victorian novel from realism, many other nineteenth-century fictions—of the adventure, ghost, "mutiny," and detective genres, for example—might also productively pull away from the strictures of a kind of novel that doesn't really exist. Examples of realism always seem to arrive with disclaimers, provisos, and qualifications, suggesting that no one can really be responsible for this critical fiction: it "wobbles," as Fredric Jameson has recently argued, caught between the paradox of affect and plot.[5] Perhaps

---

4. This trajectory is key to the work of Fredric Jameson. See *The Political Unconscious: Narrative as a Socially Symbolic Act* (London: Routledge, 2002); and *The Antimonies of Realism* (New York: Verso, 2013).

5. Jameson, *The Antimonies of Realism*, 1.

it wobbles too much. In my account, it wobbles between the antinomy of fictionality and reference, splitting off a seemingly infinite number of worlds.

In the introduction, I trace criticism of the Victorian novel from the 1850s to the 1950s, revealing a century of antidiegetic prejudice during which many Victorian novels are denounced for too much telling and not enough showing—for a decided lack of drama. Aristotle, and eventually Henry James, are the reigning spirits of this dramatic demand. The novel is somehow supposed to be a play in only a slightly different form and format. This dramatic lineage has been obscured in contemporary criticism by the idea that lyric is the dominant genre of the literary: the shift from drama to lyric is actually very recent, and it is perhaps more accurately the case that the novel and the lyric rose together as objects of literary and theoretical attention.

As this very long century ends, circa 1968, strong theories of narration and of realism give the Victorian novel critical permission to become a specifically *diegetic* (rather than dramatic and mimetic) genre.[6] It becomes realistic in a Barthesian, discursive sense. Gérard Genette's monumental work on narrative discourse allows narration to become the subject of analysis and of a kind of admiration, in that its wiles are regarded as powerful and ideologically loaded.[7] Nonetheless, throughout this period, Victorian Studies scholars maintain a sense not only of the critical past and its conflicts, but also of the formal incoherences of Victorian fiction, and of what George Levine describes as "the highly self-conscious attempt" of Victorian novelists "to explore or create a new reality."[8]

6. See D. A. Miller, *The Novel and the Police* (Berkeley: University of California Press, 1988); and Franco Moretti, *Atlas of the European Novel, 1800–1900* (New York: Verso, 1999).

7. See Gérard Genette, *Narrative Discourse: An Essay in Method*, trans. Jane E. Lewin (Ithaca, NY: Cornell University Press, 1980).

8. Levine, *The Realistic Imagination*, 2.

Similarly, Catherine Gallagher argues that English fiction becomes like French realism by the 1860s, but she argues that this is because "a culture of politics" must pull away from "a culture of facts."[9] Value moves from that which is represented to the representation itself: "The English, however, did not learn this technique from Flaubert; it followed readily from the logic of the politics of culture."[10] In Victorian Studies, we still heavily rely on both of these critics and their work, and we maintain (at least) two ideas about realism, because of the desire to partake of this newly elegant Victorian novel, because of its theoretical interest, and because of the consequential idea that this novel has laid down the law, policed us, and taught us all how to be realistic. Between historicism and narrative theory, a gulf opens. We often not only wish to ignore it, we pretend it isn't there at all.

The effect of Roland Barthes's ideas on the preterite and its profoundly cohering effects in *Writing Degree Zero*, along with Genette's spatial idea of diegesis in *Narrative Discourse*, allow for very specific ideas of narration to emerge.[11] In prestructuralist criticism, novels were typically read, in a way that becomes regarded as naive and naively realist, as continuous with the world: "The novel," Percy Lubbock writes, "with its formal outline appears for a moment, and then the life contained in it breaks out and obscures it."[12] The distance between the reader and the text falls away: inside and outside lose their boundaries. We are immersed in a "life" that includes the novel and its readers.

It is only with new ideas of diegesis as a kind of bounded space that the novel is refigured as a world in its very structure: narration crosses time and space, and the enclosure of the

---

9. Catherine Gallagher, *The Industrial Reformation of English Fiction: Social Discourse and Narrative Form, 1832–1867* (Chicago: University of Chicago Press, 1985), 249.

10. Ibid.

11. See Barthes, *Writing Degree Zero*; and Genette, *Narrative Discourse*.

12. Percy Lubbock, *The Craft of Fiction* (New York: Charles Scribner's Sons, 1921), 15.

novel begins. I argue that the stakes of this world-ing are high: it allows us to imagine that we can, in the privacy of our own minds, live in more than one world. As Johannes Fabian has suggested, ideas about modernity allow us to imagine that some primitive "others" live in a different time, a different historical moment than do those of us who inhabit modernity. Similarly, imagining that we can live in our own worlds is a high-stakes denial of what Gayatri Spivak has described as our common planetarity.[13] Theodor Adorno, in describing the alienation that produced astrology and astronomy as quackery and science, respectively, observes, "There is but one world and its division into disconnected spheres is not due to being as such, but to the organization of human knowledge of being."[14]

The figure that ruptures fiction, and our very experience of ourselves as existing in public and private worlds, is metalepsis. Gerard Genette defined this term for narrative as the breaching of "a shifting and sacred frontier between two worlds, the world in which one tells and the world of which one tells."[15] When one diegetic or ontological level intrudes into another, we are left with the vertiginous feeling that we ourselves may not be at the outermost level of narrative—on the outside, that is, but that we too "belong to some narrative."[16] The footnotes of Maria Edgeworth's *Castle Rackrent*, Sterne's plot diagrams in *Tristram Shandy*, the "scholarly apparatus" of Nabokov's *Pale Fire*, and the logically impossible staircases and hallways of Danielewski's *House of Leaves* create fissures that suggest infinite folds of space and time. And they suggest that we can imagine, and thereby inhabit, such infinities.

13. See Johannes Fabian, *Time and Other: How Anthropology Makes Its Object* (New York: Columbia University Press, 1983); and Gayatri Chakravorty Spivak, "Planetarity," in *Death of a Discipline* (Columbia: Columbia University Press, 2003), 71–119.

14. Theodor Adorno, *The Stars Down to Earth and Other Essays on the Irrational in Culture*, ed. Stephen Crook (London: Routledge, 2002), 160.

15. Genette, *Narrative Discourse*, 236.

16. Ibid.

This book is organized into a preface, an introduction, five case studies, and a conclusion. The introduction traces a turn from criticism in the everyday sense of the word, which included evaluation and open admiration or contempt to criticism as explanation and, to a surprising extent, a kind of covert admiration. The "form" of nineteenth-century fiction is created in the late twentieth century and continues to gather steam in the early twenty-first. The case studies—on the metaleptic effects of denotation, omniscience, reference, ontology, and paratext—are illustrations of ways in which the Victorian novel—like most (or perhaps all) novels—is metafictional. Fictionality is constantly ruptured by reference, although that rupture is not attended to as such: rather, the reality effect created by the presence of Napoleon or Nepal, the American Civil War or Chartism, in works of fiction ought to jolt us into an uncomfortable awareness of the impossibility of such multiple ontologies. If these novels have a "form," it is ragged and broken in its diegetic dispersion of a coherent world. In other words, it is metaleptic in that various ontological layers collapse or rupture into one another: the historical breaks into the fictional, an epigraph disturbs the text it is both inside and outside of, and the world in which the telling takes place interrupts the world of which we are being told. The quarantine between story, stories internal to stories, and the world is violated.

In the conclusion, I will revisit the critics cited by Franco Moretti in his landmark essay "Conjectures on World Literature," and read them against the grain of his argument. Moretti argues that critics from Meenakshi Mukherjee and Kōjin Karatani to Roberto Schwarz and Doris Somer similarly contend that the novels of the nations they study were pale or defective imitations of "Western" originals. This is not actually the argument of any of these critics. Henry Zhao, whom Moretti hales with particular enthusiasm, has unfortunately internalized an idea about omniscient narration that cannot be found in "Western" realism:

> Zhao [e]mphasizes from his very title—*The Uneasy Narrator* . . . the complications generated by the encounter

of western plots and Chinese narrative: "A salient feature of late Qing fiction," he writes, "is the greater frequency of narrative intrusions than in any previous period of Chinese vernacular fiction. . . . The huge amount of directions trying to explain the newly adopted techniques betrays the narrator's uneasiness about the instability of his status . . . the narrator feels the threat of interpretive diversification. . . . Moral commentaries become more tendentious to make the judgments unequivocal," and at times the drift towards narratorial overkill is so overpowering that a writer may sacrifice narrative suspense "to show that he is morally impeccable."[17]

This could be a description of the narrators of Thackeray, Trollope, or George Eliot by the earlier critics—including Henry James—whom we will meet in the introduction.

Criticism of the novel and the novel itself have given us worlds enough; the nineteenth-century novel, like those that preceded and followed it, gave us one hugely ruptured but continuous world in which we are, as imperial liberal subjects, always in more than one place at the same time, always inhabiting multiple domains in person or by proxy. Audrey Jaffe describes this odd geography:

realist fiction and its critics manifest a desire to claim the real—as territory, to use my name for *Adam Bede*'s sealing off of realist space. . . . What builds realist territory, and mediates between individual fantasies and a novel's more general ones, are conventions: devices that frame a novel's reality both for individual characters and for the novels in which we find them.[18]

17. Franco Moretti, "Conjectures on World Literature," *New Left Review* 1 (January–February 2000): 63n23. Here, Moretti is citing Henry Y. H. Zhao's *The Uneasy Narrator: Chinese Fiction from the Traditional to the Modern* (New York: Oxford University Press, 1995), 69–71.

18. Audrey Jaffe, *The Victorian Novel Dreams of the Real* (Oxford: Oxford University Press, 2016), 6.

Rather than continuing to naturalize (or simply deny) the fantasy of a coherent diegesis, we might restore the discomfort of that situation, the diegetic instability of layers of narrative folding into one layer with all of us on the inside, unsure of who narrates whom. If we displace the nineteenth-century novel from the masterful and still center of a novel history that is as contingent as the genre it tries to track, other novels might have a better chance of getting a reading that is not nineteenth-century-Anglo-Eurocentric. National or ethnic novel traditions might not be asked to follow the trajectory of a novel history that often demands a punctual arrival at and departure from realism before formal innovation can be recognized as such. The novel may not have a history at all; instead, it might have a history of readings that have created a tremendously rich set of what might be seen, from a certain point of view, as unlikely and arbitrary assemblages. There is nothing wrong with this: I would only suggest that more such assemblages might be tried out in the service of reading more novels outside of an assigned historical regimen of development that will always leave some people and places struggling to catch up in a story that might itself be a fiction.

ACKNOWLEDGMENTS

I WISH TO thank the many friends, students, and colleagues who listened to and read this book in part or in whole over the many years in which I was writing it, and the friends who sustained me. The staff of New York University's English Department—Lissette Flores, Alexandra Guillén, Alyssa Leal, Mary Mezzano, Taeesha Muhammad, Patricia Okoh-Essene, and Shanna Williams—have long been my very best colleagues and friends. Toral Gajarawala and Rajeswari Sunder Rajan were my sharpest critics and my greatest encouragers. Christopher Cannon was the most helpful and productive chair with whom I have had the pleasure to work, and now that he is off to warmer climes, he remains a deeply kind and helpful friend. Thanks to Julia Jarcho for inviting me to present part of the introduction in her graduate seminar, and for team teaching with me in the dreaded Core Curriculum. Very lately, my colleague Lenora Hanson has proved herself to be not only a brilliant scholar but a true friend. John Archer is an ally beyond compare.

My students at NYU—both at Washington Square and Wallkill Correctional Facility—have inspired me continually with their great thinking and huge hearts. I have been unusually lucky as a teacher, and it has been the very best aspect of being an academic. I want to mention especially Kimberly Adams, Durba Basu, Saronik Bosu, Alex Bright Braverman, Alicia Christoff, Vashon Cox, Lily Cui, Thurston Davis, Pier Dominguez, Eugenie Dumont, Desmond Francis, Rakeem Golson, Jermaine Haywood, Mehak Khan, Alyson Kiesel, Anjuli Raza Kolb, Margaree Little, Cate Mahoney, Grace McLaughlin, Wayne Mosley, Nicole Pasulka, Khalan Pendleton, Shawn Pettaway, Conor Spencer, Isaac Ray, Jennifer Spitzer, Omar Walker, Rachael Guyn Wilson, Eirian Yem, and Adnan Zarif. Research assistance from Saronik

Bosu, Julia Cheng, and Vashon Cox was invaluable. Heba Jahama was a crackerjack manuscript preparer at the eleventh hour; Wendy Xin is a co-copyeditor without whom I would probably never have finished this book.

Not being a very institutional person has meant that my community of colleagues is beautifully vast and dispersed. I am glad to mention here the help and friendship of Tanya Agatheocolous, Sukanya Bannerjee, Carolyn Betensky, Nicholas Birns, Aviva Briefel, Rachel Sagner Buurma, Supriyah Chaudhuri, Ian Duncan, Penny Fielding, Ryan Fong, Marcie Frank, Pamela Gilbert, Eileen Giloolly, Laura Heffernan, Nathan K. Hensley, Yoon Sun Lee, Carolyn Lesjak, Jo McDonough, Richard Menke, Elsie Michie, Mary Mullen, Clare Pettit, Adela Pinch, John Plotz, Leah Price, Talia Schaffer, Jonah Siegel, Rachel Teukolsky, Michael Tondre, and a literal giant of our field in both kinds of stature, George Levine. Cannon Schmitt is not only my dear friend but also my dear coauthor and coeditor. Working with him is not like working at all: rather, it's a kind of meeting of minds, even when we disagree.

Profound thanks to everyone who invited me to give talks taken from this project: Ian Duncan at UC Berkeley, Jay Clayton at Vanderbilt, Jill Ehnen at Interdisciplinary Nineteenth-Century Studies, the Boston Nineteenth-Century Group, including Martha Vicinus and Laura Green (who walloped me into shape!), several Modern Language Association panels, several North American Victorian Studies Association panels, including an especially helpful seminar in London, Ontario, under the leadership of Christopher Keep and Matthew Rowlinson, an American Historical Association Panel on History and Literature, Rachel Sagner Buurma and the P19 Group (Philadelphia Nineteenth-Century Group), Deidre Lynch and the Harvard Novel Theory Seminar, Supritha Rajan at the University of Rochester, Isobel Hofmyer at the University of Witswaterstrand, and Sandy Young at the University of Cape Town.

Princeton University Press has been an ideal publisher with which to work: many thanks to Anne Savarese for her acuity and efficiency, to Jill Harris for speeding me through production, and to Hank Southgate for meticulous copyediting. I am very grateful for the two anonymous readers at Princeton who were unbelievably speedy and unusually helpful in their readings of the manuscript.

The Radcliffe Institute provided an intellectual home to me for a productive year of writing this book. Judy Vishniac was a wonderful leader. Francesca Orsini helped me transform my work. Mary Franklin-Brown and Anna Zayaruznaya were great friends. Widener Library is a wonder of the world.

My friends in academia have always been there to listen to my extensive complaining and have continuously provided support, humor, drinks, and dinner: Nancy Bentley, above all, deserves a medal. Priscilla Wald and Gauri Viswanathan have been there since my first days in graduate school—we are heading for thirty-year anniversaries soon, I'm glad to say. Gina Dent helped me get through graduate school and has been there for me ever since. Nancy Ruttenberg is a true pal always. It seems like Farah Jasmine Griffin is always there and always has been there. My friend Rosemary Marangoly George was a mentor and friend who died much too young: she taught me how to respond to readers' reports, and, in general, she tried to get me to keep a civil tongue in my head. Through her I have the gift of Lisa Lowe's friendship, which is a joy.

Several younger scholars have given me the honor of being their mentors: Elaine Auyoung and Wendy Xin have become dear friends through this process. Priyanka Jacob and Ella Mershon were both a delight to work with and to know. Julia Mendoza was a graduate student when I first started teaching with her at Wallkill Correctional Facility, but she was my mentor then and she remains one now: she taught me a capacious compassion, the kind that gets you through not only a day in prison, but life in this world.

Mona Chopra is another model of compassion: she has helped me more than I can say and fixed me up more than I thought I could be fixed. I am deeply lucky to know her. Thanks to Jennifer Scott for her constant kindness, and Michele Rinaldi and Kristin Hoesl for keeping me strong. Guillaume Fourcade, Dimitri Karakostas, and Louis Gautier have made me at home in France on many occasions and with incomparable demonstrations of friendship.

Thanks to the NYU Langone Medical Center staff: from the information desk to the operating room, you all rock. To all the radiology technicians who have made me comfortable on various tables, to all the doctors and nurse practitioners who have saved my life, especially Abraham Chachoua, David Mendoza, Valerie Peck, John Golfinos, Jessica Schafrick, Michael Zervos, and Deborah Axelrod: my gratitude is boundless. The super NYU Langone nurses, who are some of the best I've ever met, watched out for me and my vital signs, gave me excellent drugs and tuna sandwiches, and walked me around, and around: I thank you. I got to finish this book because of all of you.

For over thirty years Debra Roth has been my first, best, most critical, and most loving reader. She has picked me up off the floor both literally and metaphorically; and I have basked in her exquisite appreciation for the most mundane things in life, and the most glorious. I learned how to be generous from her. Some of the choices I have made in my work life (involving picket lines and other protests) have cost her—often dearly—and yet she has always been on board with my attempts at activism. This book is for her, because of her, and whatever sentence in it you like best—she edited it, or rewrote it, or made googly eyes in the margin next to it. Thanks, Deb.

Thanks to *NOVEL: A Forum on Fiction* and Duke University Press and Edinburgh University Press for allowing me to reprint "The Novelist and Her Poor"; to *Representations* and the University of California Press for allowing me to reprint "Ghostly Reference"; and to *English Studies in Africa* for allowing me to reprint "Hetero-ontologicality, or Against Realism."

WORLDS ENOUGH

How the Victorian Novel Became Realistic (in a French Way), Reactionary, and Great

FOR A LONG time, many Victorian novels were not all that great. From Victorian critics like G. H. Lewes and Monckton Milnes in the 1850s, '60s, and '70s, to novel scholars like Dorothy Van Ghent and Barbara Hardy in the 1950s and '60s, Victorian fiction often fails to find a suitable form: it is too long, too much engaged in telling and not enough in showing, and too avoidant of the tragic in its denouements. In short, Victorian fiction is too narrative (diegetic) and not dramatic (mimetic) enough. Then, in the twenty years between 1960 and 1980, forms seemingly "native" to Victorian "realistic" fiction are found with more and more success, and the very big novel as a form lifts off, making it a naturalized effort thereafter. A new genre is born, or "read" into being in the sense that Virginia Jackson and Yopie Prins have suggested that lyric is read into being in the mid-nineteenth century and then projected backward as a long-standing poetic form, with a long-standing theoretical tradition (with Aristotle as an imagined early contributor).[1]

A newly realistic novel is born, and the novel finally gains serious prestige in the academy in the 1970s and '80s. But some of the forms we now routinely "find" in nineteenth-century fiction hinder us from taking into account a conflicted critical history in which for over a century the French and German nineteenth-century novel passed muster with British critics, but the Victorian novel was often seen as deficient, awkward, mawkish, and variously defective in form and structure. During this antidiegetic century, the demands on the novel were strictly mimetic, and Aristotelian standards reigned as if the novel were supposed to be a play in only a slightly different form and format. It was not until strong theories of narration and of realism came across the Atlantic that the Victorian novel could be assimilated to realism and achieve greatness.[2] Ironically, it is through the binary of the modernist/realist text, in which realism is the less prized kind of writing, that Victorian novels gain stature.[3] Roland Barthes's consequential idea of the referential illusion turned the novel into a discourse that had slipped its bonds to

1. See Virginia Jackson and Yopie Prins, "General Introduction," in *The Lyric Theory Reader: A Critical Anthology* (Baltimore: Johns Hopkins University Press, 2014), 1–8; and Gérard Genette, *The Architext: An Introduction*, trans. Jane E. Lewin (Berkeley: University of California Press, 1992).

2. Kent Puckett argues that it might make sense to "see narrative theory as both a powerful analytic tool and a limited expression of a historically specific and ideological world view" (*Narrative Theory: A Critical Introduction* [Cambridge: Cambridge University Press, 2016], 13).

3. D. N. Rodowick has argued that "theory" as such is "[t]utored overall by a broad binary system that opposed realism to modernism, or the classical text to the modernist écriture. . . . [Realism produces] an illusory 'reality-effect' that transparently communicates the dominant ideology in contradistinction to avant-garde practice, which working at the level of form or of the 'signifier' will reflexively interrupt this transmission. . . . [T]he presumed knowledge effect is a making visible of the ideology-effect" (*Elegy for Theory* [Cambridge, MA: Harvard University Press, 2014], 217).

any referent, and functioned, like Saussurean language, through its own system of differences.[4] Flaubert does not hunker down in central Rouen to hone his description of the place; he works on his descriptions as a problem of language—the language of realism. Genette's theory of narrative discourse involves a largely implicit presumption of the existence of diegetic consistency: although most novels break through diegetic levels, the illusion of a novelistic world is most compelling when such breakage is kept to a minimum. These structuralist "truths" about the nineteenth-century novel, as opposed to its modernist counterpart, made these novels ideological and therefore powerful, formally consistent, and great. Realism, as D. N. Rodowick writes, "communicates the dominant ideology," and it does so without letting us know that this is what it is doing.[5] Thus, realism gains formal features, wields ideological power, and is assimilated to the most "impersonal" nineteenth-century novels—those of Flaubert. The nineteenth-century novel, like other realist works (the mainstream film, realist painting), must be closed before they can be opened. Realism's formal ruse is to ignore the formal ruse, and to turn its back, to paraphrase Michael Fried on Courbet, on its audience—leaving us to "overhear" or eavesdrop on its artless world.[6] This lack of theatricality can only be thoroughly valued (or "accounted for," in the phrase of Barthes in "The Reality Effect,"[7]) in the wake of structuralism, when the minute and even boring representation of everyday life can be interpreted as significant in its very minutiae and its lack of apparent interest and value.[8]

4. Roland Barthes, "The Reality Effect," in *The Rustle of Language*, trans. Richard Howard (Berkeley: University of California Press, 1984).

5. Rodowick, *Elegy for Theory*, 217.

6. See Michael Fried, *Courbet's Realism* (Chicago: University of Chicago Press, 1990), 86.

7. Barthes, "The Reality Effect," 231.

8. See Franco Moretti, "Fillers," in *The Bourgeois: Between History and Literature* (London: Verso, 2013), 74–78.

The Drama of the Novel

Aristotle's "indivisible" or "organic" whole was revived (and misremembered) by German Romanticism in the late eighteenth century and transmitted to the Anglophone tradition by Samuel Coleridge (sometimes literally in the form of serial plagiarisms): "the fairest part of the most beautiful body will appear deformed and monstrous, if dissevered from its place in the organic Whole."[9] Compare this with Aristotle: "a beautiful object, whether an animal or anything else with a structure of parts [must give us a sense of] unity and wholeness."[10] The dramatic origins of this idea have been obscured for many of us by either Coleridge or New Criticism (or both), which has made it seem that the idea of organic wholeness derives from the analysis of lyric, and lyric alone. Mary Poovey claims that the trope of organic unity derives from eighteenth-century natural history, that "the professionalization of [literary] criticism depended upon critics' adoption of one genre in particular: the romantic lyric"; she also concurs with the standard claim that Henry James was the first critic of the novel to consider literary form.[11] But as George Kenneth Graham points out, Henry James's claims about the organic form of the novel in the 1880s would not have been news to his readers: "the Master was not really alone in the wilderness."[12] The long history of critics demanding that the novel achieve a dramatic form has been obscured by the presumed dominance of lyric in criticism and then what

9. Samuel Taylor Coleridge's *Biographia Literaria: Biographical Sketches of My Literary Life and Opinions*, ed. James Engel and W. Jackson Bate (Princeton, NJ: Princeton University Press, 1983), 234.

10. Aristotle, *Poetics*, trans. Stephen Halliwell (Cambridge, MA: Harvard University Press, 1995), 55.

11. Mary Poovey, "The Model System of Contemporary Literary Criticism," *Critical Inquiry* 27, no. 3 (Spring 2001): 422.

12. George Kenneth Graham, *English Criticism of the Novel 1865–1900* (Oxford: Clarendon Press, 1965), 113.

now seems like the rather belated struggle for the invention of a narrative form for the novel.

Novel criticism's inheritance of an Aristotelian vocabulary meant that critics had to find unity where they could, and Victorian critics very often did not find it in British novels: "the aggregate of 24 monthly pamphlets must always be disjointed and languid," opines a critic in the *Saturday Review* in 1859.[13] "[T]he whole question of unity in the novel was much debated in the 1850s and 1860s," Richard Stang writes in his study of Victorian theory of the novel. "One group of critics called for works with extremely tight structures, a limited simple plot, and a small cast of characters."[14] (In other words, a play.) Graham agrees: "the deliberate application of the principle of organic unity is one of the most remarkable and unexpected features of the whole age's criticism of fiction."[15] The French novel was often pointed to as a model: writers could stick to " 'single volumes, of modest pretensions as to size. . . . You never find a walking [walk-on?] character introduced for the sake of typifying a particular class, or an eccentric hanging loose upon the story.' "[16] *Wilhelm Meister* was another model in the view of Thomas Arnold, who ardently wished that the British novel of the mid-nineteenth century could find "the structure, the internal proportions, the various themes, yet the unity of idea, which distinguish the greatest novel that literature can show."[17] And this unity, this wholeness is specifically dramatic: even an ardent admirer of George Eliot, one who places her in "the foremost rank among contemporary

13. Qtd. in Richard Stang, *The Theory of the Novel in England, 1850–1870* (New York: Columbia University Press, 1959), 119.

14. Ibid., 115.

15. Graham, *English Criticism of the Novel 1865–1900*, 113.

16. Anonymous, "The Art of Story Telling," *Fraser's Magazine for Town and Country* 53 (January 1856): 727–31; qtd. in Stang, *The Theory of the Novel in England, 1850–1870*, 115.

17. Thomas Arnold, "Recent Novel Writing in England," *MacMillan's Magazine*, January 1, 1886, 202–9.

authors," could note in 1860 that there is a "carelessness of dramatic unity" in her work.[18] Monckton Milnes writes in a review of *Middlemarch*, "Strictly speaking, the writer should be as little seen in person in a novel as he would in a modern drama."[19] Seriousness and depth are also often found wanting: W. C. Roscoe "found Thackeray's novels marked by 'thinness and superficiality.'"[20] Walter Bagehot finds Scott's characters superficial. R. H. Hutton chastises Trollope for not having "the heart (shall we say the nerve?) to ruin Lady Glencora" and give *Can You Forgive Her?* "a genuinely tragic interest."[21] He is finally satisfied with *He Knew He Was Right*, calling it "a tale of truly tragic jealousy."[22] When Eliot is praised unconditionally, it is because her "novels are not novels in the ordinary sense of the term— they are really dramas: as the word is understood when applied to *Hamlet* or the *Agamemnon*."[23]

Henry James is still too often imagined as the first theorist of the novel, bursting on to the scene with his essay "The Art of Fiction," which appears in *Longman's* in 1884 as a riposte to a not very coherent, or typical, essay by Walter Besant of the same name.[24] James makes a set of moves that will become

18. Anonymous, "George Eliot's Novels," in *The Rambler* (London: Burns and Lambert, 1861), 4:80, 99.

19. See Monckton Milnes's review in *Edinburgh Review* 137 (January 1873): 126–35, 134. Leslie Stephen is one of the few fans of authorial intrusion: "One main advantage of the novel . . . is precisely that it leaves room for a freedom in such matters which is incompatible with the requirements of dramatic writing. . . . I like to read about Tom Jones and Colonel Newcome; but I am very glad when Fielding or Thackeray puts his puppets aside for the moment and talks to me" (qtd. in Graham, *English Criticism of the Novel 1865–1900*, 123).

20. Stang, *The Theory of the Novel in England, 1850–1870*, 52.

21. Richard Holt Hutton, "*Can You Forgive Her?*," *Spectator*, September 2, 1865, 979; qtd. in Stang, *The Theory of the Novel in England, 1850–1870*, 57.

22. Richard Holt Hutton, "*He Knew He Was Right?*," *Spectator*, June 12, 1869, 707; qtd. in Stang, *The Theory of the Novel in England, 1850–1870*, 58.

23. "Felix Holt—The Radical," *Westminster Review*, October 1866, 200; qtd. in Stang, *The Theory of the Novel in England, 1850–1870*, 47.

24. See Mark Spilka, "Henry James and Walter Besant: 'The Art of Fiction' Controversy," *NOVEL: A Forum on Fiction* 6, no. 2 (Winter 1973): 101–19.

familiar in criticism for the next century: he condescends to the Victorian novel as having no theory or consciousness of itself, he ignores the existence of Victorian criticism, he damns the intrusive Victorian author, and he argues that morality, which Besant admittedly only mentions in passing, is too much of an issue in Anglo-American letters: the timidity of the English novel is its "moral" problem. This combination of assertions and omissions sets the modernist critical stage in a very particular way: the Victorian novel does not take itself seriously enough. Trollope's self-effacing intrusive narrator is metonymic of this problem:

> He took a suicidal satisfaction in reminding the reader that the story he was telling was only, after all, a make-believe. He habitually referred to the work in hand (in the course of that work) as a novel, and to himself as a novelist, and was fond of letting the reader know that this novelist could direct the course of events according to his pleasure.[25]

There is no critical past with which to grapple—the English novel has not yet become what James describes as "*discoutable*"— despite a tradition of literary criticism of fiction stretching back to the Romantics; the problem with discussing literature in general is, unsurprisingly, Victorian prudishness.[26]

Ever since James, Victorian criticism has been repeatedly forgettable. And yet James's criticism of the novel was part of a well-established dramatic lineage in British novel criticism in the Victorian period. His dislike of Trollope's authorial intrusions is precisely in the vein of this tradition, in which such intrusions are seen as constituting a break in the dramatic unity of the novel. The relationship of the Victorian novel to drama has been wonderfully adumbrated in David Kurnick's analysis

---

25. Henry James, *Theory of Fiction*, ed. James E. Miller Jr. (Lincoln: University of Nebraska Press, 1972), 175.

26. As excellent a critic as Kevin Ohi has recently followed this line of thinking almost verbatim. See "'The Novel Is Older and So Are the Young': On the Queerness of Style," *Henry James Review* 27, no. 2 (2006): 140–55.

of Thackeray, Eliot, and James as novelists haunted by their failure as dramatists. Kurnick brilliantly observes that many of the devices we see as native to the novel and as the nuts and bolts of its vaunted representation of "interiority" are instead, or perhaps also, dramatic: "interior monologue, free indirect discourse, and the careful restriction of point of view" are all ways of dramatizing the self even as they may be ways for exploring its depths.[27] For Kurnick, "these devices smuggle the memory (or more properly the fantasy) of the crowded theatrical space into the psychic interior."[28] I think they also work to answer the demands of critics who wanted drama—as we have seen—quite literally, in the novel. Novels were to be watched, not listened to, imagined as performed, not thought of as narrated. Victorian novel theory is antidiegetic: it is profoundly, unapologetically, self-consciously mimetic, in classical terms. The "naive" realism of the nineteenth century was never that: it was Aristotelian, and dramatic, and James was part of a lineage—somewhere in the middle of it, rather than at the beginning of it. Marcie Frank, in *The Novel and the Repertory*, makes a detailed case for the strong and transitive relationship between the theater and fiction from the Restoration through the eighteenth century, in which the drama and the novel were constantly learning from one another: "The status of letters in novels affects the ways letters are used on the stage in the eighteenth century; likewise the demise of the soliloquy and the increased frequency of the aside can be explained in terms of the widening sphere of the novel's influence."[29] It is curious that in nineteenth-century criticism, the traffic seems to be all in one direction: from tragedy to novel, or from a previous theatrical practice and theory that the novel takes over.

27. David Kurnick, *Empty Houses: Theatrical Failure and the Novel* (Princeton, NJ: Princeton University Press, 2012), 11.
28. Ibid.
29. Marcie Frank, *The Novel and the Repertory 1680–1814* (Lewisburg, PA: Bucknell University Press, forthcoming).

Mid-Century Forms: Tragedy
and Henry James

Many mid-twentieth-century critics struggle to find a form for Victorian fiction that tries to move beyond but cannot quite free itself of the heritage of dramatic theory. The critics I discuss here—Dorothy Van Ghent and Barbara Hardy—are central to this struggle and bracing in their admissions of failure, or their accusations of failure on the part of Victorian novels. The focus of their titles on form—Van Ghent's *The English Novel: Form and Function* (1953), Hardy's *The Novels of George Eliot: A Study in Form* (1959), and *The Appropriate Form: An Essay on the Novel* (1964)—seems to announce a program that must be urgently accomplished, a kind of Marshall New Critical Plan for the novel, which is indeed a popular object of study for the many new and "untraditional" (i.e., older and less affluent) college and university students in attendance in the post–World War II period.[30] The works themselves often concede that many nineteenth-century novels are a tough fit for various formal demands on the novel: tragic and Jamesian ones, chiefly.

Van Ghent hews closely to dramatic tenets: the novel "can use all sorts of discursive methods that the drama cannot use. But it employs dramatic method most liberally, for it represents human beings *as if* in tangible space and time, that is 'scenically' placed and related."[31] Unafraid to evaluate, or part of a culture of criticism in which evaluation is still part of the job, Van Ghent dismisses many of the novels she discusses as failures or partial failures usually because they avoid the imperatives of tragedy: *Clarissa*, *The Heart of Midlothian*, and *The Egoist*, for example, all fail to make the cut. Van Ghent asserts that "the

30. See the preface to Homer Obed Brown, *Institutions of the English Novel from Defoe to Scott* (Philadelphia: University of Pennsylvania Press, 1997).

31. Dorothy Van Ghent, *The English Novel: Form and Function* (New York: Holt, Rinehart and Winston, 1966), 3; emphasis in original.

genius of tragedy is the same as the genius of comedy. It is what Cervantes knew, whose great comic hero, Quixote, walks in the same shades with Orestes and Oedipus, Hamlet and Lear. It is what Moliere knew. Even Jane Austen knew it."[32] Van Ghent adeptly subsumes all kinds of novels under the rubric of tragedy, including ones that have been thought of as comic. Indeed, in her readings, every successful novel shows us something absolutely terrible about the world, including *Pride and Prejudice*, in which Austen, "ambushed by imbecility," demonstrates how characters must work out their lives in a language based on a "savage theology of 'property.'"[33]

Perhaps Van Ghent's clearest connection to the dramatic method is her abhorrence of the "omniscient author convention" (note the word "author," a Victorian holdover).[34] Thackeray's "technique of omniscient authorship can allow a relaxed garrulity and what James called 'the terrible fluidity of self-revelation.'"[35] For Van Ghent, his comments in *Vanity Fair* are "inane and distracting" and make for "two orders of reality . . . clumsily getting in each other's way: the order of imaginative reality, where Becky lives, and the order of historical reality, where William Makepeace Thackeray lives."[36] This "sound track," as Van Ghent describes it, tears the novel apart ontologically, breaking up its form, and distracting the reader from the "world" of the novel, where world "is the nearest similitude for a novel."[37] George Eliot in *Adam Bede* does the same thing. In the questions for study and discussion that make up the second

32. Ibid., 237.

33. Ibid., 111.

34. Ibid., 143.

35. Ibid., 139. Henry James comments on Victorian intrusive omniscience many times; in Trollope he calls it "little slaps" at the illusion of reality and then "suicidal." Henry James, "Little Slaps at Credulity," in *Theory of Fiction*, 175; "Anthony Trollope," in *Partial Portraits* (Ann Arbor: University of Michigan Press, 1970), 116.

36. Van Ghent, *The English Novel*, 139.

37. Ibid., 6.

half of the book, Van Ghent asks, or comments with a question mark, "Do you feel that the convention of the 'omniscient author' is actually the right one for this book, or do you feel that is the only one adequate for the materials, but that George Eliot has allowed it too much license?"[38]

It is important to note here that there are, historically, two very different forms of omniscience, and Wayne Booth famously described and deconstructed them in *A Rhetoric of Fiction* (see "Rehabilitating Omniscience" below). The Victorian novel is, at a certain point, annexed to a structuralist idea of French realism, which is imagined as free of intrusive narration. These combined critical moves regularize the Victorian novel into something less interesting and less problematic than what it had been for previous generations of more skeptical critics, or critics for whom that novel was not yet great.

Great Expectations and *Wuthering Heights* achieve greatness for Van Ghent because they do not indulge us: Dickens gives us a world "where human encounter is mere collision," and Brontë gives us one in which we find a "nakedness from the web of familiar morality and manners."[39] Both are redeemed by form: plot in *Great Expectations*, and first-person (dramatic) narrative framing in *Wuthering Heights*. The ultimate value of the novel, Van Ghent writes, in what seems like the kind of bland phrase we might (unfairly) associate with 1953, is "its ability to make us more aware of the meaning of our lives."[40] But this is not bland in Van Ghentian practice. Van Ghent asks us to understand Moll Flanders as the "progenetrix of the wasteland, sower of our harvests of technological skills, bombs, gadgets, and the platitudes and stereotypes and absurdities of a morality suitable to a wasteland world."[41] She tells us that the "heir" of Dickens's " 'century of progress' is the twentieth-century concentration camp, which

38. Ibid., 402.
39. Ibid., 189.
40. Ibid., 7.
41. Ibid., 43.

makes no bones about people being 'things.' "[42] Her demand for
tragedy is an ethical one; she reads novels as histories of the hor-
rific present.

Barbara Hardy's attempt to explain the form of Eliot's fiction is an understandably tortured effort to make a case for "her
power of form, a striking but relatively disregarded aspect of
her work as a novelist."[43] Hardy's touchstone for form is, unsurprisingly, tragedy: "it is true," she writes, "that in the nineteenth
century, the novel becomes the medium of tragedy."[44] Tragedy is
the subject of four out of eleven chapters of *The Novels of George
Eliot: A Study in Form*.[45] It is enough to show that a novel is a
tragedy or has tragic elements to prove that it has a form. Hardy
admits that it might be argued that "Eliot always evades the
tragic conclusion" (Van Ghent would say so), and Hardy, to her
credit, doesn't fully resolve this problem, except to argue that
"the heroines" are tragic figures. This is part of Hardy's characteristic impatience with the idea that perfect or consistent form
is a value in itself. Indeed, she associates strict form with drama
and with a perversely dramatic use of the novel: the " 'organic'
forms [of Henry James] lack the graduation of the natural
organism, for he is . . . luxuriating in difficulties which arise necessarily in the drama but which are a more gratuitous discipline
in the novel."[46]

Hardy begins to think about the problematic "omniscient
author convention" and to understand and recuperate it in
various ways, the most interesting being the idea that "Eliot is
a social reformer who places her sympathetic plea outside her
characters, showing them realistically as too dumb to plead or

42. Ibid., 128.
43. Barbara Hardy, *The Novels of George Eliot: A Study in Form* (New York:
Oxford University Press, 1959), 1.
44. Ibid., 32.
45. "The Unheroic Tragedy"; "The Tragic Process: *Adam Bede*"; "The Tragic
Process: The Heroines"; "The Tragic Process: The Egoists."
46. Hardy, *The Novels of George Eliot*, 30.

too charmless to attract."[47] Thus the need for the talkative narrator (author), who steps in to explain people who cannot explain themselves. Hardy also tries to render the drama novelistic instead of asking the novel to be dramatic:

> Eliot's scenic method is as varied as her other means of presenting character and developing action. The scene can serve the double purpose of narrative and theme, often providing a visual resting-place. Her scenes are of course not all scenes of crisis, though it is the status of the scene as symbol which I am concerned with here. In most of the novels there are a large number of scenes which are not even essential to the development of plot, but which familiarize us with the character before that character is set in tragic action.[48]

Hardy makes a case here for narration itself as a literary form deserving of attention and approbation, rather than as a defect of presentation: to defend scenes that are not "essential to the development of the plot" is still a fairly controversial gesture when Hardy is writing. The idea of the "visual resting-place" suggests a novelistic theater in which we can pause and listen to the narrator, imagining a scene in our heads, as Victorian narrators so often ask us to do.

In *The Appropriate Form: An Essay on the Novel,* Hardy gets quite energetic about batting away the dramatic requirements foisted on the novel by the tradition of Jamesian criticism, and more actively and less defensively makes a case for the "expansive novel":

> We still use . . . Jamesian formal standards with little qualification in our own analysis. We insist that the large loose baggy monster has unity, has symbolic concentration, has patterns of imagery and a thematic construction of character, and in the result the baggy monster is processed by our New

47. Ibid., 17.
48. Ibid., 185.

Criticism into something strikingly like the original Jamesian streamlined beast.[49]

Hardy goes on to make a strong case for everything that is *not*
unified, concentrated, and patterned: "Economy can be mean
and waste generous."[50] In her reading of *Middlemarch*, Hardy
cheerfully and aggressively argues that "its realism and its unity
are flawed."[51] It is for Hardy a sexually dysfunctional novel, in
fact. The narrator is explicit about Casaubon's impotence, she
argues, but does not give us, in Ladislaw, a structural opposite
in potency, or general sexiness. The reticence of the novel about
sex is out of kilter with its lack of reticence about everything
else, and even the reticence about sex is restricted to Ladislaw,
in whom "sensibility acts as a surrogate for sensuality."[52] This
imbalance destroys unity, or James's " 'law' that the antithesis
[between characters] should be direct and complete."[53] But the
final line of the chapter puts paid to Henry James and his strict
structural requirements: "Who would exchange the flawed *Middlemarch* with its omissions made conspicuous by its suggestive
reticence, for a novel where truth were reduced and mere aesthetic balance retained?"[54] And I would ask, who now would
call *Middlemarch* "flawed"? Although we imagine that we don't
engage in such evaluation any longer, perhaps we should understand the places where we evaluate without using specifically
laudatory or deprecatory language. Perhaps evaluation now
resides in the celebration of form, as if writers have achieved
something we know in a more perfect state. It might be excit-
ing to seek, from a different vantage critically and historically
than that of Hardy, the "flaws" of novels we now treat as nearly

49. Barbara Hardy, *The Appropriate Form: An Essay on the Novel* (London:
Athlone Press, 1964), 7.
50. Ibid., 39.
51. Ibid., 108.
52. Ibid., 125.
53. Ibid., 121.
54. Ibid., 131.

perfect structures, if only to admit how random our canonical inclusions and exclusions are, and how many works we exclude from the greatness list are excluded for faults that the included works suffer (or benefit) from quite widely.[55]

Rehabilitating Omniscience

In 1961, Wayne Booth disrupts the dramatic lineage of novel criticism by asserting that showing is always telling and that telling is a kind of showing: "the author can never choose to disappear."[56] Shockingly, but in a telling move about showing, in the very first paragraph of the preface to *The Rhetoric of Fiction*, Flaubert becomes a kind of Trollopian author who is unfavorably compared to James:

> Is there any defense that can be offered, on aesthetic grounds, for an art full of rhetorical appeals? What kind of art is it that will allow Flaubert to barge into his action to describe Emma as "unaware that now she was eager to yield to the very thing that had her so indignant," and as "totally unconscious that she was prostituting herself"? Whatever their answers, critics have often been troubled by this kind of overt, distinguishable rhetoric.[57]

55. An interesting example is Masao Myoshi discussing Ōgai's novel *The Wild Goose*: "The narrative structure . . . is a bit awkward, a frequent problem with Japanese novels. The narrator, Okada's friend, begins by reminiscing on past events, but soon disappears from the tale, almost making it a third-person story. He returns in Chapter 18 when it becomes increasingly clumsy to present events which the narrator cannot have been in a position to know" (*Accomplices of Silence: The Modern Japanese Novel* [Berkeley: University of California Press, 1974], 48; qtd. in J. Keith Vincent, *Two-Timing Modernity: Homosocial Narrative in Modern Japanese Fiction* [Cambridge, MA: Harvard University Press, 2012], 56). This is very much like the narrative structure of *Madame Bovary*, which begins with a first-person and then morphs into a third-person narrator, and then changes back into a first-person narrator at the novel's end.

56. Wayne C. Booth, *The Rhetoric of Fiction* (Chicago: University of Chicago Press, 1961), 20.

57. Ibid., xiii.

Booth immediately points out that James's dramatic presentation is also "rhetorical." It may be "disguised," but there is always a narrator at work and always a rhetoric of narration in a novel. Indeed, the "rhetoric of fiction" is, largely, narration. Taking on James, and what "Jamesians have made of James," Booth goes on to argue, famously, that telling produces a stable, and good, irony, while showing produces an unstable and bad irony. This defense of telling is perhaps what has made *The Rhetoric of Fiction* both a monument in novel studies and less influential than it might otherwise have been: it renders a clumsy judgment on narrative technique (about which it is otherwise hugely subtle). Perhaps what is more important is that Booth maintains the historical distinction between the intrusive *author* and the "objective" narrator, even though both seemed to be subsumed under the "implied author."[58] Booth tries to keep two kinds of omniscience in play. This is one of the major oddities of the Victorian novels that must be extinguished for the Victorian novel, and realism at large, to become great.

J. Hillis Miller deals a direct and lasting blow to the dramatic tradition in his well-known pronouncements on omniscient narration, which, he calmly tells us, is not omniscient and not exactly narration. It is "not an anonymous storyteller . . . but the role of the collective mind."[59] Miller makes the intrusive, busybody, antidramatic narrator the "determining convention" of Victorian fiction instead of its major blight.[60] The narrator is indeed in the world of the story: "immanent rather than transcendent."[61] We move from having an author who is an actual historical person, or, less bodily, an "implied narrator," as

58. See the section on "Reliable Narrators as Dramatized Spokesmen for the Implied Author" in ibid., 211–14.

59. J. Hillis Miller, *The Form of Victorian Fiction: Thackeray, Dickens, Trollope, George Eliot, Meredith, Hardy* (1968; repr., Cleveland: Arete Press, 1979), 63.

60. Ibid., 63.

61. J. Hillis Miller, *Thomas Hardy: Distance and Desire* (Cambridge, MA: The Belknap Press of Harvard University Press, 1970), 14.

Booth would have it, within the diegesis to having a narrator who is a misty collective mind floating about invisibly—it is a big leap; existential subtleties replace ruptured worlds:

> There are few places where the narrator explicitly confesses that the novel is a novel, though many aspects of the narrative language may implicitly recognize this. For the most part, the narrators of Victorian novels talk as if they were confronting directly or in historical retrospect a world independent of their knowledge of it, but a world over which they happen to have extraordinary powers.[62]

Miller describes a very particular Victorian narrator: this is not an eighteenth-century self-reflexive narrator, or a postmodern wisecracking narrator, or a modernist godlike narrator, paring her fingernails. The Victorian narrator might be implicitly metafictional, but in general it is objective about reporting on an intact world that it did not make, a world that is really "there" somewhere, and this not-quite-solid collective mind is in it. There is a mystical feeling to much of what Miller writes about the Victorian novel and how it works: this narrator, who has become so important to us, is particularly wispy.[63]

Less quoted than Miller's formal remarks about omniscient narration are the "reasons" for it. The first nine pages of his chapter on narration, "Narrator as General Consciousness," chart the isolation, loneliness, and social failure of Dickens, Eliot, Trollope, Hardy, and Meredith. "To be an outsider looking in, however, is not yet to be a novelist. . . . The transformation which makes a man [*sic*] a novelist is his decision to adopt the role of the narrator who tells the story."[64] But not any kind of narrator. "The characteristic work of each of these novelists comes into existence when he chooses to play the role not of

---

62. Ibid., 65.

63. A JSTOR search for "Hillis Miller" AND "omniscience" turns up 160 hits, including 14 since 2010, suggesting the ongoing prestige of his formulations.

64. Miller, *The Form of Victorian Fiction*, 62.

a first person narrator who is an actor in the drama, and not even the role of an anonymous storyteller who may be identified with an individual consciousness, but the role of a collective mind."[65] Dramatic representation is highly individual; the form of Victorian fiction is collective, or is about trying to be part of a collective. It is about loneliness transformed into incorporation. Miller is specifically antidramatic *and* antilyrical in his brief for the omniscient narrator as a legitimate literary figure/form: the Victorian novel is about relations, and characters realize themselves in relation to other characters and not in "contemplation of rocks, trees, and daffodils."[66] The difficulty here is the one cited earlier: Miller does not account for the chattiness and intrusiveness of the Victorian omniscient author. Collective minds do not say "I" and interrupt the action to muse on their ideas about narrative, or to dream, or to judge a character, or to tell you what they are leaving out of the story. This is very much an individual, a "personal" voice in J. Hillis Miller, a position that will be ironically reinforced by D. A. Miller's very serious modification, in this case citing Austen as the impersonal narrator par excellence (ignoring, apparently, her startlingly intrusive conclusions, in which the narrator says "I" and washes her hands of her annoying characters):

> Nowhere else in nineteenth-century English narration have the claims of the "person," its ideology, been more completely denied. Hence, the staring paradox of Austen's narration: it is at once utterly exempt from the social necessities that govern the narrated world, and intimately acquainted with them down to their more subtle effects on character. It does not itself experience what it nonetheless knows with all the authority of experience.[67]

65. Ibid., 63.
66. Ibid., 5.
67. D. A. Miller, *Jane Austen and the Secret of Style* (Princeton, NJ: Princeton University Press, 2003), 32.

D. A. Miller insists on a more radical impersonality than does J. Hillis Miller, making the nineteenth-century narrator yet more omniscient and extradiegetic.

But J. Hillis Miller's imagining of the Victorian narrator as collective and continuous allows Victorian fiction to be realistic in a French sense (also a critical invention)—which is to say, "objective," and Miller is a key figure in this transformation, although he is decidedly not a structuralist. In the chapter called "The Ontological Basis of Form," Miller asserts that there are three key questions for the interpretation of Victorian fiction: realism, intersubjectivity, and time. And yet, Miller does not make us think or feel that the Victorian novel is realistic, especially not *Our Mutual Friend*, which he takes (perhaps ill-advisedly) as one of his major texts in this chapter. He reads in detail the following passage from the second chapter of the novel in which "the great looking-glass" becomes an agent of representation and "reflects the table and company. Reflects the new Veneering crest, in gold and eke in silver. . . . Reflects Veneering, forty, wavy-haired, dark, tending to corpulence, sly, mysterious, filmy."[68] Miller writes,

> Each adjective in the sentence is like a magic formula bringing miraculously into existence in the reader the quality it names. As each is added to the last Veneering gradually manifests himself like an ectoplasmic vision at a séance, hovering in the space behind the mirror, a space which is both the imaginary space of the novel and the inner space of the reader's mind. The mirror mirrors nothing, but generates its own images out of that nothing.[69]

Characters become embodied as spirits do at seances, which is to say not at all. We are watching something that is nothing.

68. Charles Dickens, *Our Mutual Friend*, ed. Adrian Poole (New York: Penguin Books, 1997), 21.

69. Miller, *The Form of Victorian Fiction*, 40–41.

We are behind the mirror; we are in our minds and in the space of the novel. The geography and ontology here make me long for a medium (or an intrusive narrator) to guide me through the seance, and to create some signage for the spaces that are of the novel and of my mind. Indeed, *Our Mutual Friend* sounds very much as if it could have been written by Virginia Woolf in Miller's account, suggesting that the form of Victorian fiction may not be as period-specific as we would all like it to be.

"Form" is finally relation, in Miller's account. Miller finds in novel endings a great pathos for himself as a reader cut adrift from all the relations about which he has read, finally shut out from a world he can never quite reach, turned back to the reality from "the other side of the looking glass":

> The silence after the last word of the novel, like the silence after the last note of a piece of music, is by no means the silence of triumphantly perfected form. It is rather a stillness in which the reader experiences a poignant sense of loss, the vanishing of the formative energy of the work. This secret source of form was never reached while the novel continued, but was held open as a possibility toward which each page separately reached. . . . When the novel is over the sense of that possibility is lost, and this generates a feeling of nostalgia, of regret for having lost the last glimpse of a marvelous country which can be seen afar not when . . . the novel is over, but only while it is going on in its continuous failure to be perfect or perfectible.[70]

The form of Victorian fiction is a possibility, a continuous failure, a desire, an almost, an other country. It could be likened to a performance in a theater, but a performance of music and not of a play (because it is narrated, but not by an embodied actor). But still, the curtain comes down, the lights come up, and the spectator is no longer part of the collective, until he starts to

70. Ibid., 48.

turn the pages of another novel, again filled with hope, again ending in grief.

Narration Theory

To briefly recapitulate the argument thus far: for Victorian critics through Van Ghent and Hardy, the Victorian novel is a problem. It isn't great yet. The intrusive omniscient narrator, the lack of unity, and the swerve away from tragedy make it difficult to defend on ethical and aesthetic grounds. Wayne Booth tries to rehabilitate the intrusive omniscient narrator by making all narrators intrusive authors, giving us the "implied author," a concept that has little in the way of staying power precisely because this narrator is going to be disappeared by criticism. J. Hillis Miller, in 1968, ignores the critical legacy (and many women critics of considerable stature) and invents a new Victorian novel (literally! see the notes to the book: he cites none of the critics of Victorian fiction that have come before him). He doesn't do this alone, of course. He's part of a movement and moment (the advent of "French" theory, in Miller's case, phenomenology) in which the novel (along with pyschonalytic and Marxist criticism) is gaining ground in terms of its prestige. But he is a key figure in transforming Victorian omniscience into something more in keeping with modern omniscience, and in ignoring the difficult critical history surrounding this turn. At the same moment, a transhistorical narrative theory develops, and we then have one kind of omniscient narration, rather than the idea of "intrusive" versus "objective" variants of this style that are peculiar to the nineteenth and twentieth centuries respectively. This allowed for the development of a smoother, more formally impressive "realism." In the following case studies, I would like to experiment with undoing this realism and reading Victorian fiction as formally ragged. It is remarkable that until the 1960s, the Victorian novel was not great in the sense that it is now. And it did not have a theory of its own most important feature: narration.

It takes a strong theory of narration and a strong theory of realism to make the Victorian novel great and realistic. I am going to discuss a highly selective list of what I call narration theorists, including Roland Barthes, Gérard Genette, D. A. Miller, and Fredric Jameson, who I think are the main figures in the diegetic turn, although many others could be adduced. I am then going to try to account for the present moment in theories of Victorian reading (both reading as performed by Victorians in novels and readings by us of these Victorians) in the work of Leah Price, Nicholas Dames, and John Plotz.

The most important aspect of the arrival of narrative theory is the arrival of a theory of narration, which means the rehabilitation of diegesis from a few thousand years of the domination of mimesis. Genette's ideas are more often used than cited: they have become so "true" and "obvious" in narrative theory that they are almost naturalized aspects of the form: it would be like citing Lukács every time nineteenth-cenutry realism were mentioned. The diffusion of Genettian diegesis naturalizes terms that have since been widely deployed to create or discover the critical fiction of the realistic novel as a foil for Proustian modernism.[71]

71. In a characteristic effort to keep the tangled ontology of realism apparently seamless, the narrative theorist Monika Fludernik cites a passage from *Narrative Discourse* concerning metalepsis in Balzac's *La Vielle Fille* and asserts that what Genette (and many others) would regard as rupture between narrative levels—when Balzac's narrator in *La Vielle Fille* enters (with the reader) the home of the widow Cormon—leaves the characters in the scene "to attend to their business elsewhere" (Gérard Genette, *Narrative Discourse: An Essay in Method*, trans. Jane E. Lewin [Ithaca, NY: Cornell University Press, 1980], 134). Fludernik argues that Balzac's narrator adds to the "realistic illusion of story-world representation . . . aiding the narratee's . . . imaginative immersion into the story rather than foregrounding the metafictional and transgressive" (Monika Fludernik, "Scene Shift, Metalepsis and the Metaleptic Mode," *Style* 37, no. 4 [Winter 2003]: 383). Fludernik does not justify this claim: her opinion seems to rest on the idea that Balzac is a realistic writer, and therefore this entrance of the reader and narrator into the diegesis is not metalepsis but immersion. This is a common reading of metalepsis in "realistic" fiction: the text is closed,

Genette is not responsible for this: he does recognize metalepsis in several nineteenth-century novels, and it may indeed be later critics who—implicitly or explicitly—periodized a kind of stability of diegetic levels in the nineteenth century.

Genette borrowed a new idea of diegesis from the filmologist Étienne Souriau and remediated it for literary narrative in the 1960s. For Souriau, diegesis is "all that belongs by inference to the narrated story, the world proposed or supposed by the film's fiction."[72] (Christian Metz will say it is the "denotated world of the film.")[73] Genette repurposes this term for fiction: for him, the diegesis

> is indeed a universe rather than a train of events (a story) (here he distinguishes his term—a different word in French than the one Plato used—from Plato's, in which diegesis is narrating in one's own character versus mimesis, which is story-telling in a dramatic mode); the diegesis is therefore not the story but the universe in which the story takes place—universe in the somewhat limited (and wholly relative) sense in which we say that Stendhal is not in the same universe as Fabrice.[74]

---

enclosed by the idea of diegesis—an idea thoroughly naturalized in narrative theory. Fludernik uses what is now a popular term in narratology: "storyworld," extending the "world" of earlier critics and also creating a kind of membrane around realistic fiction: diegesis is thus reified (383). Following Barthes's dissolution of the "referential illusion," we might remove the diegetic illusion: the idea that there is a storyworld at all may prevent us from perceiving various kinds of metalepsis—not only the intrusions of narrators and readers into the narrative, but also a kind of indexical aspiration that haunted many eighteenth-century writers, and may be resurgent in the paratexts that we treat so gingerly in the nonreflexive "realist" novel.

72. Étienne Souriau, *L'univers filmique* (Paris: Flamarrion, 1953), 7; qtd. in Claudia Grobman, *Unheard Melodies: Narrative Film Music* (Bloomington: Indiana University Press, 1987), 21.

73. Christian Metz and Michael Taylor, *Film Language: A Semiotics of Cinema* (Chicago: University of Chicago Press, 1974), 98.

74. Gérard Genette, *Narrative Discourse Revisited*, trans. Jane E. Lewin (Ithaca, NY: Cornell University Press, 1988), 17–18.

Genette makes diegesis not only about space rather than process or person (i.e., who tells the story and in what persona), but about levels or layers: diegetic levels are key to his narrative theory: universes can nest within universes in his "relative" definition.

The second idea is that realism, via Barthes, is a discourse and not a rough or brilliant or too-detailed or fantastic transcription of a readily available social reality. In *Writing Degree Zero*, perhaps the first high-impact work of French Structuralism on Anglo-American novel criticism, Barthes points out the power of the past tense, that is, of narration:

> The world is not unexplained since it is told like a story; each one of its accidents is but a circumstance, and the preterite is precisely this operative sign whereby the narrator reduces the exploded reality to a slim and pure logos . . . finally the preterite is the expression of order, and consequently of a euphoria. Thanks to it, reality is neither mysterious nor absurd; it is clear, almost familiar, repeatedly gathered up and constrained in the hand of a creator. . . . For all the great storytellers of the nineteenth century, the world may be full of pathos but it is not derelict, since it is a grouping of coherent relations.[75]

Realism—through telling, that is, through narration—organizes the social world rhetorically, making what would otherwise be mysterious into something "coherent," at least temporarily. Narration is a kind of ideological cement, producing both euphoria and a well-organized pathos. Steven Marcus, a very "early adapter" of *Writing Degree Zero*, points out that

> reality within this system of consciousness tends to be represented as recollection; it is remarkably stable, and its laws of both expression and development appear to arise

---

75. Roland Barthes, *Writing Degree Zero*, trans. Annette Lavers and Colin Smith (New York: Hill and Wang, 2012), 36–37.

immanently, and once again, "naturally," out of the material it selects as its content rather than out of the consciousness that selects the material. . . . It offers assurance to its society of readers because the world it represents has already been defined and in some sense closed off; things in it . . . *have already happened.* And in this respect one of its central purposes is the purpose of control.[76]

The closed-off, already over world of the British novel might be usefully compared to what Mary Mullen terms "anachronism" in a group of nineteenth-century Irish novels, which have hardly achieved the ability to control the past, and thereby can only indicate the future with an unnerving but liberating uncertainty:

> Mobilizing relationships between past and present, aesthetics and history, Unionist and anti-imperial politics, history in Edgeworth's Irish writing exceeds the forms through which she attempts to organize it. In the process, her writing questions the impulse towards a useful history, showing that particulars—aesthetic experience, the contingencies of timing, the peculiarities of an Irish context—help imagine political possibilities that work against the assumed future that a useful history presupposes and literary history often secures.[77]

In my argument, British writing can no more control the "contingencies of timing" than can Irish writing, but we accept the anomalous in Irish writing simply because it's Irish and unable to claim control of "European form."

D. A. Miller and Fredric Jameson enhance the power of "European" narrative techniques in their work, increasing the

76. Steven Marcus, "Human Nature, Social Orders, and 19th Century Systems of Explanation: Starting In with George Eliot," *Salmugundi* 28 (Winter 1975): 25.

77. Mary Mullen, "Anachronistic Aesthetics: Maria Edgeworth and the 'Uses' of History," *Eighteenth-Century Fiction* 26, vol. 2 (Winter 2013–14): 236.

prestige of narration once more. In one of what seems like Miller's most personal essays—on David Copperfield—he raises the idea that "David might be any David"—even David Miller.[78] This seemingly random and purely subjective thought takes on steam as the chapter progresses: David might be any David because there is no one home subjectively in the novel. In trying to hide themselves from the violence of the social order, even first-person narrators are evacuated of content and become pure forms, available shells to be inhabited at will. First-person narration cannot solve the problems of omniscience because it is always already the third person: it is always "doing the police." The ideological success of the nineteenth-century narrator lies in its detachment from subjectivity—even when that narrator speaks in the first person. David Copperfield, D. A. Miller argues, has no face, no identity, no status as the "hero" of his own story. Character and narrator split apart, leaving subjectivity distributed socially—a condition from which the reader hopes she can exclude herself because she suffers neither the condition of character-hood nor that of being narrated: this indeed is the point of being extradiegetic.

In Jameson's work, narrative can almost engage the Lacanian Real, which hides just out of sight but not outside of the allegorization of social conflict novels produce. Narrative dreams of solutions (as did the face paintings of the Caduveo analyzed by Lévi-Strauss that we cannot accomplish outside the novel).[79] But they remain powerfully available for the utopian imagination. This process is perhaps most pronounced for Jameson in science fiction, in which the novel imagines new worlds: they present us with "archaeologies of the future" that offer us various scenarios that we might now still have the power to choose from,

78. D. A. Miller, *The Novel and the Police* (Berkeley: University of California Press, 1988), 192.

79. See Fredric Jameson, *The Political Unconscious: Narrative as Socially Symbolic Act* (Ithaca, NY: Cornell University Press, 1982), 77. See also Claude Lévi-Strauss, *The Savage Mind* (Chicago: The University of Chicago Press, 1966).

a power or agency that is always receding as the future comes to greet us with flood and fire.[80] But fictional narrative—the narration of the imagined past or imagined future—is powerful because it gives us potential access to both the unconscious and to the Real, otherwise inaccessible realms. Thus narration is not only powerful in Jameson; like David Copperfield and his fellow Dickens characters, it is empty of subjectivity and filled with a collective unconscious that knows more than any of us can know individually, or in the extradiegetic reality of everyday life. It is notable that, unlike Mullen and many scholars of the non-European novel, Jameson can only find truly utopian possibilities in a largely American, entirely male catalogue of sci-fi writers.

The nineteenth-century narrator is reimagined by these critics, transformed from the realistic-world-shattering chatterbox derided by Henry James and Dorothy Van Ghent: the narrator of Miller and Jameson is almost ideology itself, an ideological state apparatus by many other names, who doesn't barge in, but rather whispers in a mixed language of character and world, leaving us suspended between power and abjection, yet in what can still seem like a strikingly solid social place. The ideology of form, to borrow Jameson's storied phrase, creates forms in which to think and live, many of which threaten a kind of existential incarceration in the plots of the past.[81]

In recent work on the nineteenth-century novel, critics readily notice the disruptions I am writing about in this book. However, they tend to write about them as thematizations of reading or narrating, rather than as problems of writing or disruptions of the formal coherence of these novels. Indeed, we might say they pick up the dramatic tradition of novel criticism in different

80. See Fredric Jameson, *Archaeologies of the Future: The Desire Called Utopia and Other Science Fictions* (London: Verso, 2005), esp. chap. 5, "The Great Schism."

81. See Jameson's "On Interpretation: Literature as a Socially Symbolic Act," chap. 1 in *The Political Unconscious*.

terms: readers and their props—books—become the subject of attention, as if we are largely, in reading novels, observing the fictional uses of books. Over a decade ago, Leah Price wondered if it were not "too crude to hypothesize a shift from 'reading' as a noun used to describe the product of the speaker's own ruminations . . . to 'readings' as an activity delegated to others by a critic who describes it from a safe historical distance."[82] If it was too crude then, it certainly isn't now: we have a veritable raft of work in both book history and affect theory in which the activity of reading is the critic's chief concern.[83]

Price should perhaps be credited with inaugurating this shift. She has debunked, in two books and several articles, many of our more cherished ideas about the virtues and consistencies of Victorian reading habits. The anthology, for example, "trained readers to pace themselves through an unmanageable bulk of print by sensing when to skip and where to linger."[84] Novels were read by Victorians in a "culture of the excerpt."[85] More recently, in *How to Do Things with Books in Victorian Britain*, Price points out that books are often as absorbent as

82. Leah Price, "Reader's Block: Response," *Victorian Studies* 46, no. 2 (Winter 2004): 231–42.

83. See, for example, Stephen Arata, "On Not Paying Attention," *Victorian Studies* 46, no. 2 (Winter 2004): 193–205; Andrew Elfenbein, *The Gist of Reading* (Stanford: Stanford University Press, 2018); Debra Gettelman, "The Victorian Novel and Its Readers," in *The Oxford Handbook of the Victorian Novel*, ed. Lisa Rodensky (Oxford: Oxford University Press, 2013), 111–28, as well as her articles on George Eliot ("Reading Ahead in George Eliot," in "Victorian Structures of Feeling," special issue, *NOVEL: A Forum on Fiction* 39, no. 1 [Fall 2005]: 25–47) and *Jane Eyre* ("'Making Out' *Jane Eyre*," *ELH* 74, no. 3 [Fall 2007]: 557–81); Kelly Hager, "Estranging *David Copperfield*: Reading the Novel of Divorce," *ELH* 63, no. 4 (Winter 1996): 989–1019; and "Jasper Packlemerton, Victorian Freak," *Victorian Literature and Culture* 34, no. 1 (2006): 209–32; and Elisha Cohn, *Still Life: Suspended Development in the Victorian Novel* (Oxford: Oxford University Press, 2016).

84. Leah Price, *The Anthology and the Rise of the Novel: From Richardson to George Eliot* (Cambridge: Cambridge University Press, 2000), 5.

85. Ibid.

they are absorbing (as sandwich-wrappers, for example). More seriously, Price argues,

> What once took place on the level of discourse now migrates to the level of story. Instead of an editor's paratextual jokes breaking into the narrative as in *Tristram Shandy*, now a book throw by one character breaks into the text read by another. The violence of book throwing at the level of story replaces the violence of frame breaking at the level of discourse. Replaces, or at least supplements: for every time a novel reminds us of the sensory attributes of the object we're holding—and by extension, reminds us of our own eyes and our own hands—it shatters our concentration as violently as John Reed or Miss Murdstone breaches David's or Jane's. John aims the book to avoid breaking windows, but book throwing still ruptures the transparency of mimesis.[86]

Price both maintains the canonical view of the realist novel—that it is not ruptured—and simultaneously admits, vividly and boldly, that it most certainly is. Throwing books makes them material, and pulls us from text back to book, from story world, to a world that includes both readers of and in books.

Nicholas Dames makes a very similar argument, with the help of what he refers to as "neural science," calling attention to the way that Victorian writers of various kinds call attention to the oscillating attention and inattention of readers.[87] Thackeray, for example, "deflates the scene"[88] of Amelia's parting from Sedley with the intrusion of an extradiegetic fictional reader JONES, "who reads this book at his Club, will pronounce to be excessively foolish, trivial, twaddling, and ultra-sentimental.

86. Leah Price, *How to Do Things with Books in Victorian Britain* (Princeton, NJ: Princeton University Press, 2012), 77.

87. Nicholas Dames, *Physiology of the Novel: Reading Neural Science, and the Form of Victorian Fiction* (Oxford: Oxford University Press, 2007), 77.

88. Ibid., 75.

Yes; I can see Jones at this minute . . . taking out his pencil and scoring under the words 'foolish, twaddling,' etc., and adding to them his own remark of '*quite true.*' "[89] This is an especially striking case of a narrator disturbing the reader's absorption: a finicky fictional reader residing in another fictional space reads what Thackeray writes him thinking and then underlines his own thoughts—as written by Thackeray. What could be more distracting than such a multileveled ontology in which agency is distributed across diegetic layers and free indirect discourse becomes literal. JONES underlines his own thoughts because he agrees with them; their origin is in the narrator's invention of JONES and his cantankerous consciousness.

John Plotz has offered the term "semi-detachment" for the kind of mental state the British provincial novel induces, allowing readers to be both at home and in a larger world as they read.[90] His example, from *The Mill on the Floss*, suggests how the novel induces this state. For now, I want to note that this novel has a first-person omniscient narrator who seems, like Pip or Jane Eyre, to be telling the story of her own life, but of course cannot be, since Maggie Tulliver does not survive the novel. But this is someone who knows the literal place of the novel, the banks of the Floss River near the tributary called the Ripple, or it is someone who used to know this place: "I remember those large dipping willows. I remember the stone bridge."[91] A new paragraph, the second of the novel, begins:

> And this is Dorlcote Mill. I must stand a minute or two here on the bridge and look at it, though the clouds are threatening, and it is far on in the afternoon. Even in this leafless time of departing February it is pleasant to look at—perhaps the

89. William Makepeace Thackeray, *Vanity Fair: A Novel without a Hero* (New York: Penguin, 2003), 12.

90. John Plotz, *Semi-Detached: The Aesthetics of Virtual Experience since Dickens* (Princeton, NJ: Princeton University Press, 2018).

91. George Eliot, *The Mill on the Floss*, 3rd ed. (Oxford: Oxford University Press, 2015), 7.

chill damp season adds a charm to the trimly-kept, comfortable dwelling-house, as old as the elms and chestnuts that
shelter it from the northern blast.[92]

This description goes on for three paragraphs and culminates
when the narrator spots a "little girl" with a "queer white cur."[93]
The final paragraph of the chapter brings the narrator/author
back to her desk:

> Ah my arms are really benumbed. I have been pressing my
> elbows on the arms of my chair, and dreaming that I was
> standing on the bridge in front of Dorlcote Mill, as it looked
> on February afternoon many years ago. Before I dozed off, I
> was going to tell you what Mr and Mrs Tulliver were talking
> about, as they sat by the bright fire in the left-hand parlour,
> on that very afternoon I have been dreaming of.[94]

Plotz characterizes this narrator as undergoing a "phase shift,"
a term from mathematics meaning the change of the phase of
the oscillation of a wave, and the term is useful for his focus on
attention and detachment.[95] My formulation is more extreme,
and less focused on reading: I am interested in the world-
breaking mode of this narration: that is, metalepsis. The narrator slowly brings us into a world the narration of which may be a
dream; it may be a memoir (but whose?); it may be a novel with
a strange narrator, a first-person extradiegetic narrator who can
do all the things omniscient narrators do, including free indirect discourse, and have full knowledge of the insides of characters' very subtle minds and psychological states. This is a very
precise individual mind, but also a mind with a strong affective
investment in the narrated world, which is continually ruptured
by this unknown, extradiegetic I. This is also—a point that will

92. Ibid.
93. Ibid., 8.
94. Ibid., 8–9.
95. Plotz, *Semi-Detached*, 107.

become important in case study 3—a novel whose paratextual epigraph becomes an intradiegetic epitaph by the novel's end. The novel begins and ends with the same words, but their ontological shift suggests the permeability of the limits of the novel.

All of these recent critics notice the formal heterogeneity of the Victorian novel, and they argue, rather gently and largely implicitly, against the generic or narratologically boundaried novelistic world that structuralism and narrative theory recommend. This seems to me characteristic of a widely engaged practice in Victorian Studies and nineteenth-century novel studies more broadly, in which ideas that are useful—realism, diegesis, form—are retained even as critics understand and admit, with admirable candor, how problematic they are. The Victorian novel, on the most cursory inspection, is riddled with the key features of metafiction, although it is certainly rarely, if ever, accused of this, and it is conspicuously absent from discussions of metafiction that often begin with *Tristram Shandy* and then leap to the postmodern novel without pausing anywhere along the way. The Victorian novel is what narratologists characterize as a "standard" narrative.[96]

If we read the Victorian novel as something other than realistic, we find a fiction that, like the formally inventive fictions that surround it on all temporal sides, allows for radical ontological flexibility. Dorothea Brooke is like Don Quixote as we meet him in the epigraph from *Middlemarch*; we can easily imagine that she has also read *Don Quixote*, and that is why she is like him, just as the Don is like the romance characters he has read. We inhabit, perhaps as a character ourselves, an infinite regress of characters who have become characters because of other characters.

The geography of Victorian Britain was inconceivable: an overseas empire that found continual but always piecemeal presentation and representation in illustrated periodicals and

96. Uri Margolin, "Reference, Coreference, Referring, and the Dual Structure of Literary Narrative," *Poetics Today* 12, no. 3 (Autumn 1991): 517–42.

in the exhibits of the Great Exhibition, in sunburnt returning civil servants and in tea, in novels, and in ivory buttons. As we practice, in our novel reading, the connecting and then breaking apart of worlds, we can inhabit multiple, "non-adjacent diegetic environments."[97] At least all of us who are reading such novels and listening, still, to those narrators, those authors, and what they think, the ones that remind us that we are resting our arms on the ledge of a stone bridge and on the arms of our chair, at home and in an invented space where there is an open circuit between fiction and the world created by paratexts, garrulous narrators, and problems of fictions that create reference. We are deciding word by word what is fantasy and what is history, and we can readily imagine historical and fictional characters inhabiting the same spaces because we are inhabiting those spaces with them. Van Ghent did not feel comfortable in 1953 about this ontological open circuit, but the normativization of the Victorian novel has made such ontological maneuvering an unproblematic, because unacknowledged and unconscious, practice in the late twentieth and early twenty-first centuries. The novel is no longer the genre of homelessness described by Lukács, but one that the last forty years of criticism has helped to make us feel at home everywhere and in multiple domains at the same time, although this "we" keeps getting smaller and smaller as the ubiquity of homelessness and statelessness in our world makes education, study, reading, and thinking the precincts of the very few.[98] That is part of the ironic triumph of novel worlds: we make them, as we use our planet, according to a plot that ends in extinction.

97. Kurnick, *Empty Houses*, 103.
98. See George Lukács's theory of transcendental homelessness in *Theory in the Novel: A Historico-Philosophical Essay on the Forms of Great Epic Literature*, trans. Anna Bostock (Boston: MIT Press, 1971).

Denotation

HOW DOES WHAT we call realism recuperate reference in the realm of the fictional, offering a kind of epistemological safety net for the awkward and awful stuff it regularly represents? We might imagine that the novel as a genre is set up to provoke these questions: it provides an open circuit between fictionality and reference that can never be closed. But only in the age of realism, and in the realistic works that continue to be written in its modernist and postmodernist wake (realism remains the dominant mode of the novel, especially at the level that comes to be defined as "middle brow," even in the midst of these literary innovations), do we critics believe so firmly and earnestly in reference. We usually don't say that; we think about "realism" and absorb the problems of Barthes's "referential illusion" under that generic tarpaulin. But this open circuit provides a denotational metalepsis: a rupture of one level into another— the realm of the factual and the material into the realm of the fictional.

In the eighteenth, twentieth, and twenty-first centuries, reference may be everywhere in the novel, but it is everywhere undermined: by satire, parody, and self-reflexivity. Realism is the form that requires that we think about the ways in which the fictional is like the real, and the real like the fictional. It asks us to decide what is historically accurate and what is purely or only fictional on a case-by-case basis: Is Jane Eyre a typical governess? Is Kim a typical Irish orphan in nineteenth-century Lahore (if there can be such a thing)? Are Elizabeth Gaskell's laboring class characters authentic, and if so, in which features of their lives and selves? These questions provoke various kinds of critical answers, but they do not usually ask us to think about metalepsis: that is, the way in which the object world of the novel not only connotes, but also denotes—taking us away from the novel and toward other sources of information if an object is obscure, provocative, or seems in some way meaningful that we cannot readily determine.

Cannon Schmitt, in his reading of maritime fiction, has developed a method of literal reading that is corrective or supplementary to my own in *The Ideas in Things*. Instead of proceeding from fiction to history (as if that were a known route), Schmitt recommends a "literalism that is not a materialism: its trajectory does not move from texts to objects in history and back again; rather it traces a textual circuit that begins and ends in fiction but dwells between times among dictionaries, nautical charts and tide tables."[1] We should get ourselves caught up not only in texts, as we usually think of them, but in things like tables and charts. In his reading of tides in Conrad's *Heart of Darkness*, Schmitt suggests not only the bibliographic sublime offered by unfamiliar words and terms, but a chance at maritime moonlighting for serious, adventurous readers of this fiction— fiction that has often been seen as not serious because it is about adventure. I will try to continue with this method in this case study, examining a particularly recalcitrant marine referent: ballast.

1. Cannon Schmitt, "Tidal Conrad (Literally)," *Victorian Studies* 55, no. 1 (Autumn 2012): 16–17.

Generic Weight

"Stone ballast is the most thoroughly ignored object category in shipwreck archaeology, and for good reason."[2] When I first came across this note, it was spread across two pages and the first half of the sentence up to "and for good reason" had me in high spirits. I thought I had found scholars who could explain this stuff to me. But instead, I hit the same dead end that I kept hitting doing this research. The historian Lauren Benton even sent me to a shipwreck salvage expert who could help very little. This is an unstudied, uninteresting category of the material, and for that reason, I was hooked on pursuing it even in the most roundabout ways.

In the first comprehensive manual on stowing cargo in ships, Robert White Stevens's *On the Stowage of Ships and Their Cargoes*, we can learn the proper packing of everything from ale to zinc, and lists of goods and articles considered by various customs authorities as most liable to infection including lute strings and goats' hair. Stevens defines ballast as "a quantity of iron, stone or gravel, or some similar material, deposited in the hold when there is no cargo or too little to bring the ship sufficiently low in the water."[3] Ralph Davis, in *The Rise of the English Shipping Industry*, tells us that "[t]o the ship owner the two most important questions to be asked about a commodity have always been, How far is it to be carried? And how much does it weigh? It was, paradoxically, not the heavy good but the handful of important ones like cotton which were exceptionally light that caused the most difficulty in the operation of ships."[4] And here is Joseph Conrad on the subject in his memoir *The Mirror of*

2. From a footnote in D. H. Keith and Joe J. Simmons III's article, "Analysis of Hull Remains, Ballast, and Artifact Distribution of a 16th-Century Shipwreck, Molasses Reef, British West Indies," appearing in *Journal of Field Archaeology* 12, no. 4 (Winter 1985): 416–17.

3. Robert White Stevens, *On the Stowage of Ships and Their Cargoes* (London: Longman's, 1858), 79.

4. Ralph Davis, *The Rise of the British Shipping Industry* (London: MacMillan, 1962), 175.

the Sea: "There are profitable ships and unprofitable ships. The profitable ships will carry a large load through all the hazards of the weather and when at rest will stand up in a dock and shift from berth to berth without ballast. I have never seen that sort of paragon myself, but I have seen these paragons advertised amongst ships for sale. . . . It is open to any man to say that his ship will sail without ballast; and he will say it too, with every mark of profound conviction, especially if he is not going to sail her himself. The risk of advertising her as able to sail without ballast is not great, since the statement does not imply a warranty of her arriving anywhere. Moreover, it is strictly true that most ships will sail without ballast for some little time before they turn turtle upon the crew."[5]

Ballast is generic weight; it circulates species, specimens, and potential commodities accidentally. It creates random migration and random value. Ballast is waste matter that can suddenly become precious: the mahogany in empty slave ships returning to England; the whale bone detritus used by bored sailors to create scrimshaw; the cowry shells that become the currency of the West African slave trade. Ballast contains biological matter that can create disturbance and disaster: larvae and microorganisms picked up in one port and then dumped in another change or destroy environments—the zebra mussels currently clogging up the Great Lakes, for instance.

Species and commodities find new homes and new uses: a ship full of tagua nuts used as ballast arrives in Germany from South America in the mid-nineteenth century and becomes "vegetable ivory," the stuff of faux ivory buttons and baubles. Button manufacturers like to tell a neutral story about these nuts (seeds, actually):

> During the mid-1800s, trade routes between Europe and South America started flourishing. Wooden sailboats were used to carry export goods and passengers. The sailboats

5. Joseph Conrad, *The Mirror and the Sea* (New York: Doubleday, 1921), 46.

were filled with sand in the bottom to add stability while traveling in a rough sea. But there was a major flaw to this strategy. The wooden ships would often rot or get destroyed around the hull which caused leaks and water got filtered onto the sand. The sand would absorb the water which made the ship sink. The sailors started looking for a substitute and got a solution for this flaw in the tagua nuts. Tagua nuts were heavy and plentiful and did not absorb water. These nuts were used as ballast for years in the ships and proved to be helpful.[6]

Some tagua seeds landed in Hamburg, and an artist happened to put a few nuts in his pocket and started carving them, and soon enough a huge button business was born.[7] Historians tell of the bonded indigenous labor that made extraction of such products from the upper Amazon basin possible: the tagua nut does not figure on the same scale as rubber and oil, but the labor process was the same.[8]

Ballast confuses archaelogists regularly: did the sixteenth-century participants in the Frobisher expeditions smelt iron, or are the iron blooms found in the sand there counterweights for ship repair or ballast from Norse or Russian ships?[9] Algonquins in what is now Westchester County, New York, made implements with flint that came as ballast from British ships. F. Peter Rose, an amateur archaeologist, warns beachcombers and scholars alike to "temper their enthusiasm with careful

6. "The Evolution of Corozo Buttons through Tagua Nuts," Corozo Buttons, posted July 10, 2014, http://www.corozobuttons.com/2014/07/evolution-corozo -buttons-tagua-nuts/.

7. Ibid.

8. See Soren Hvalkof, "Outrage in Rubber and Oil: Extraction, Indigenous Peoples and Justice in the Upper Amazon," in *People, Plants, and Justice: The Politics of Nature Conservation*, ed. Charles Zerner (New York: Columbia University Press, 1999), 112.

9. Millions of dollars have been spent, so far to no avail, to answer this question. See William W. Fitzhugh and Jacqueline S. Olin, *Archaeology of the Frobisher Voyages* (Washington, DC: Smithsonian, 1993), 221–28.

research before announcing their extraordinary find."[10] It might well derive from a "humble ballast heap."[11]

Ballast keeps a ship just heavy enough to stay the right way up and stay on course; it comes to figure the stuff of reference and evidence, and also, in the nineteenth century, it suggests a key component of character—that which keeps one from being flighty. It also makes the ship an object of intentional extremes. Ships, after all, carry their cargoes and passengers deliberately, and keep the record in a nicely explicit form—the manifest. But a ship traveling "in ballast" is often considered to be empty, and the matter of ballast is often, in fact usually, not recorded. Ballast is latent, but it is not a part of the cultural unconscious. It is, rather, part of the environmental history of oceans and coasts, a history that is only beginning to be considered in the new subdiscipline of environmental marine history. But like the unconscious and like history, it will have to be tracked as an absent cause: tracked backward from its effects.

Ballast does not fit into any category of existing thing theory. It is not a commodity, certainly not a gift or a fetish, but neither is it an unmolested thing in the sense described by either Arjun Appadurai or Bill Brown—that is, an object living a social life unsullied by the relations that tend to reduce and restrict things for human use and exchange.[12] Ballast is, most of the time, opaquely generic, only starting into specificity when it becomes money. In one of ballast's most startling transformations, cowry shells from the Maldives, used as ballast for centuries by Arabs and Europeans, became the currency of West Africa and of the slave trade:

> Long before our era the cowry shell was known as an instru-
> ment of payment and a symbol of wealth and power. This

10. F. Peter Rose, "A Flint Ballast Station in New Rochelle, New York," *American Antiquity* 33, no. 2 (April 1968): 243.

11. Ibid.

12. See Arjun Appadurai, *The Social Life of Things: Commodities in Cultural Perspective* (Cambridge: Cambridge University Press, 1986); and Bill Brown, introduction to *Things*, ed. Bill Brown (Chicago: University of Chicago Press, 2004).

monetary usage continued until the 20th century. If we look
a bit closer into these shells it is absolutely not astonishing
that varieties as the *cypraea moneta* or *cypraea annulus*
were beloved means of payments and eventually became in
some cases huge competitors of metal currencies. All characteristics of money, i.e. durability, handiness or convenience,
recognizability and divisibility are embodied in these small
shells. In comparison with foodstuff or feathers which can
fall prey to vermin, shells withstand easily frequent handling.
They are small and very easy to transport and their alluring
form and looks offer them a perfect protection against forg-
ery. Besides, counting was not always absolutely necessary.
As the shells almost all had the same shape and size weigh-
ing often sufficed to determine the value of a payment.[13]

An entirely neutral stuff like sand or water becomes like gold in
one part of the world, the part where slaves are another unusual
kind of freight, and as Ian Baucom has detailed in *Specters of
the Atlantic*, a kind that can be thrown overboard as insured
goods whose value is completely disconnected from their physical, never mind their human, being.[14] Slaves are not ballast:

13. "Cowry Shells, a Trade Currency," National Bank of Belgium, posted
January 11, 2007, http://www.nbbmuseum.be/en/2007/01/cowry-shells.htm.
Cf. Jan Hogendorn and Marion Johnson, *The Shell Money of the Slave Trade*
(Cambridge: Cambridge University Press, 1986).

14. Ian Baucom quotes, in *Specters of the Atlantic: Finance Capital, Slavery,
and the Philosophy of History* (Durham, NC: Duke University Press, 2005),
from John Weskett's *A Complete Digest of the Theory, Laws and Practice of
Insurance* (1781) to delineate the basis on which drowned slaves become more
valuable than sick ones: "Average and contribution are synonymous terms in
marine cases and signify a proportioning of loss to the owner's goods thrown
overboard in a storm. When goods arrived damaged, the first thing requisite is,
to find out the true quantum of the damage or loss, or the diminution of value
which have sustained and *to apportion that loss or what would have been the
value of the goods if they had arrived safe and undamaged*" (Baucom, *Specters
of the Atlantic*, 108; emphasis added). We see why sick slaves were dumped
as damaged goods: more insurance could be collected on the loss than on the
"damaged goods."

indeed, they are the opposite extreme: they are so infested by the money form that their commodification, and their status as insured commodities, overrides every other possible facet of their subject- or object-hood. Ballast is at the other end of value flexibility: at one moment, cowry shells are the unnamed weight in the hull, seemingly endlessly available in the Maldives; at the next, they are a legitimate and recognizable currency, exchangeable for slaves. However, history does not stint on examples of human ballast: Irish refugees from the Famine in Canadian lumber ships were little more than human ballast packed into the holds of these freight vessels; similarly, many emigrants to Australia had a function in ships that had delivered wool to Britain, whose owners were happy to have an even minimally paying outward-bound cargo.

In this case study, I want to explore three conditions of things and of reference: the shipshape, the off-shore, and the ballastic. "Shipshape" comes to describe a very upright and neat condition outside of boats and ships only in the mid-nineteenth century when, as Helen Rozwadowski points out in her history of deep-sea exploration, there was a dramatic increase in knowledge about the sea and when working at sea and sea travel— for pleasure or for emigration—became a much more common Anglo-American experience across social classes.[15] It suggests that shipping and ships had earned a high level of esteem in the national imaginary and that the activities on ships were seen as more legitimate, more routine, less dangerous, and less piratical, by the mid-nineteenth century, than they had been previously. This was also the time when the shore became a place of leisure. Also by the mid-nineteenth century, British ships had been free of slaves for about a generation. They could be imagined as ethical commercial spaces, although, as Jonathan Lamb has described the sociality of the ship, "the law of self-preservation

15. Helen M. Rozwadowski, *Fathoming the Ocean: The Discovery and Exploration of the Deep Sea* (Cambridge, MA: Harvard University Press, 2008).

is both the bond and solvent of" its "social microcosm."[16] We know, from the massive literature of the sea, how volatile the heterotope[17] of the ship is and how it can provide for us, as C. L. R. James says of *Moby Dick*, a world in which we can live in the extremes of the characters and their situations.[18]

My use of the shipshape describes the perfectly planned and ordered space. Sol Gills's ship's instruments shop in *Dombey and Son* is shipshape, as if about to sail away, compacted and "screwed together" as if it might break apart on shore, where the currents of social relations are perhaps as violent as the currents of the sea. *Dombey and Son* is a typical Victorian domestic novel: it is about a family that is also a shipping firm, except we don't see any shipping in the novel. We see goods piling up on docks, and we see the effects of wealth (not good), but we do not see the labor that produces the wealth that produces Dombey and Son, firm and family. We only see the ship's instruments in Sol Gills's shop and the iron hook that replaces Captain Cuttle's hand—a hand given up to the sailor's trade, we assume: bitten off by a shark, or lassoed by a rope, or perhaps frostbitten during a watch. The fishily named Gills and Cuttle are the moral center of this novel: Sol Gills has a shop shaped like a ship; Captain Cuttle is a man who seems to have become a ship (and/or an ink-secreting shellfish—a novelist?): he is "oaken," and his shirt collar is described as a sail beneath his neck.[19] They are shipshape characters, and Sol's instruments, which are out of date—made for sailing rather than for steam vessels—are packed together

16. Jonathan Lamb, *Preserving the Self in the South Seas, 1680–1840* (Chicago: University of Chicago Press, 2001), 165.

17. See "What's It About?," Heterotopian Studies, updated 2019, http://www.heterotopiastudies.com/whats-it-about/, for an exploration of Foucault's idea of the heterotope as unstable, almost impossible physical arrangements.

18. See C. L. R. James, *Mariners, Renegades, and Castaways: The Story of Herman Melville and the World We Live In* (1953; repr., Hanover, NH: Dartmouth College Press, 1985).

19. Charles Dickens, *Dombey and Son* (1848; repr., Harmondsworth: Penguin Classics, 2002), 29 and 136.

in the most rational, most space-saving, most jostle-free way imaginable:

> The stock in trade of the old gentleman comprised chronometers, barometers, telescopes, compasses, charts, maps, sextants, quadrants, and specimens of every kind of instrument used in the working of a ship's course, or the keeping of a ship's reckoning, or the prosecuting of a ship's discoveries. Objects in brass and glass were in his drawers and on his shelves, which none but the initiated could have found the top of, or guessed the use of, or having once examined, could have ever got back again into their mahogany nests without assistance. Everything was jammed into the tightest cases, fitted into the narrowest corners, fenced up behind the most impertinent cushions, and screwed into the acutest angles, to prevent its philosophical composure from being disturbed by the rolling of the sea. Such extraordinary precautions were taken in every instance to save room, and keep the thing compact; and so much practical navigation was fitted, and cushioned, and screwed into every box (whether the box were a mere slab, as some were or something between a cocked hat and a starfish, as others were) . . . that the shop itself, partaking of the general infection, seemed almost to become a snug, sea-going, ship-shape concern.[20]

Nothing can come between these objects: they are compact to the point of being molecularly bonded, as is the relational world of Sol Gills's shop and extended family, which includes his nephew Walter Gay and his friend Captain Ned Cuttle. A snug, all-male ship of a shop and family, cut off from the present, uncommercial because uncustomed. It stands in radical opposition to Dombey and Son, in which there is too much commerce and too many women. It is, in short, a fictional enterprise within a fiction, one that Dombey must prop up with

20. Ibid., 46.

charitable cash. But it is also a common fantasy, a Dickensian twist on a common genre: a maritime fiction within a domestic one—a ship in a bottle. The twist, however, is significant: only a doubly fictional ship that is resolutely landlocked can be a fully rational and intentional concern, in a shop that is actually a museum financed by a shipping magnate. The moral center of the novel, in other words, is a fantasy: a ship without the violence of the actual maritime world, or the violence recorded congenially in Captain Cuttle's hook—which he kisses in farewell to ladies and unscrews and replaces with a knife at mealtimes—and which is just one more thingly part of his very thingly but very comfortable and functional self. Indeed, the shipshape figures a utopian object world. Captain Cuttle, as a hybrid human/fish/thing, is a particularly fine steward in a world of things, with apparently no use or exchange value, that have settled into snug and seemingly uninterruptible relations with one another.

The ballastic is the opposite of the shipshape: it figures the random, the irrational, and the unnamed whose effects turn up at intervals that can span generations, ages, and epochs. "Ballastic" is an adjective I've coined to describe its literal and metaphorical possibilities in the social lives of things: it signifies at once contingent identity, referential blockage, and unrecorded arrival.

Ballast is resiliently generic. It is also, I think, emblematic of the highly specific terminology of the sea that maritime fiction uses without explanation, and often without glossary, footnote, or other paratextual assistance; that is to say, it is a term that blocks as much as it names. Margaret Cohen writes that "the dramatic energy of the plot [of maritime fiction] hangs on the activity of sailing a ship as performed by its captain and crew."[21] This activity takes place in what she calls "active description" in

21. Margaret Cohen, "Traveling Genres," *New Literary History* 34, no. 3 (Summer 2003): 485.

which nautical terms "are introduced as if they were obviously
known to readers; with no gesture towards their possibly spe-
cialized status. The readers' familiarity with them is assumed,
as if she too followed the sea; sometimes these terms take center stage at dramatic high points, indicating actions central to
the outcome of the plot."[22] For example, as Dickens notes of the
instruments in Sol Gills's shop, none but the initiated can guess
what their uses might be. And so as top-gallant yards luff and
sailors jump over taff-rails and the patent log rings and a buster
blows, the landlubber reader reads along with little idea of
what is going on beyond the sense that men are struggling with
nature, laboring mightily for their survival against the weather
and the sea with a technology the vocabulary of which is infinitely evocative because it is opaque. The reading experience
for most of us might be described as radical reality effect; the
words have a certain denotative savor, I would argue, because
they are all signifier with no signified and with no referent. This
literal-figurativeness, with no referential interference, creates
what I would like to call "off-shore-ness"—the displacement of
a kind of factual fiction to the vast ocean, the distant river, the
imagined sea—to the extraterrestrial space in which laws and
meanings can be improvised by pirates, parliamentarians, and
readers alike.

Seafaring fiction is the ballast of the landlubber type. If the
terrestrial novels of the nineteenth century famously ignore labor
and scant class violence and imperial exploitation, salt-water
narratives tell literal stories of labor, of global exploitation, of
class and race violence, and of fatally consequential hierarchies
and divisions of labor. But by floating them on various bodies of
water, they are removed generically from the realm of the realistic. Maritime fiction reports on a reality most readers will never
see, or will encounter perhaps briefly as passengers, museum
goers, or most likely of all, as readers. The representations of

22. Ibid., 489.

the social world in such fictions are, in the argument of Pierre Bourdieu, "total and null": the work of art "brings unreality to what it presents as reality."[23] C. L. R. James argues in his reading of *Moby Dick*, in *Mariners, Castaways and Rebels* (written while he was interned on Ellis Island for Communist activities), that we have on board the *Pequod* in 1851 a highly specific and highly prescient portrait of global capitalism: white American management, and an international working class composed of a South Seas "savage," a native American, and an African.[24] The nobility of the crew is in their work, he contends, and the insanity of the captain and the mates derives, in large part, from their parasitism on the labor of others and their consequent leisure time to acquire and indulge neuroses. If the labor of the laboring class is redeemed in *Moby Dick*, it is also represented in all of its class-ridden violence. We can see, or rather vaguely glimpse, our real social relations in the characteristic haze of "off-shore-ness"— haze being Conrad's favorite weather for storytelling.[25] We don't have to see directly, and we don't have to actually believe the violence that we see. A favorite critical complaint about maritime fiction is that it is not credible: this is also probably its greatest redemption as fiction that openly confesses the political unconscious so expertly and so precisely.

What kind of language signifies without creating a signified or a referent? This is a stronger reality effect than that of Barthes, for whom the reality effect bypasses the signified in hot and extinguishing pursuit of the referent. Nautical language tends to extinguish signifieds *and* referents and arrive nowhere except the everywhere of dead metaphors, or rather, metaphors that have never lived for many of us: we trim our sails, we take a different tack, we are or aren't worth our salt, we batten down

23. Pierre Bourdieu, *The Field of Cultural Production: Essays on Art and Literature*, ed. Randal Johnson (New York: Columbia University Press, 1993), 159.

24. See James's chapter on "Fiction and Reality," in *Mariners, Renegades, and Castaways*, 69–89.

25. Joseph Conrad, *Heart of Darkness* (New York: Penguin, 2012), 3, 1.

the hatches, we get three sheets to the wind, and we say, giving probably no thought to lobster traps, that we are "all set"—
without having any idea what many of these metaphors refer to
in nautical practice. In my book on things in Victorian fiction, I
found it readily possible to bring reality effects back into contact
with their historical signifieds—or what I understood to be their
historical signifieds.[26] I tried to produce historical narratives of
things that change the texts in which they were lodged. Ballast
does not yield to this method. The resonant anecdote about ballast does not give way with more research: the trail goes cold
almost immediately. In a kind of referential analogue, we can look
up all the parts of a ship that figure in a dramatic moment in
Conrad, Melville, Marryat, or Stevenson, but we cannot make
ourselves see, as Conrad would have it. The nautical reality effect
is a genuinely opaque effect that gestures toward a real that we
cannot visit, or that we cannot visit sufficiently to make the signi-
fiers stick to signifieds and referents—to resonate with the reality
that they denote so percussively. Perhaps this is why the maritime novel often figures itself as romance, and why the sea was a
romance as well as an economic necessity for many young men
in the nineteenth century. Melville describes first-time sailors in
Typee as "long-haired, bare necked youths, who, forced by the
united influences of Captain Marryat and hard times, embark
at Nantucket for a pleasure excursion to the Pacific."[27] This is
also why such fictions can represent men doing the actual work
of ships, against the weather and the ocean, practically killing
themselves in broken-down wrecks of ships. These are men that
are getting every last penny, franc, and farthing wrung out of
them, in a near-perfect analogy to the often-fatal factories and
mines of the same historical moment. Despite all this, these fictions remain romances. These are ethnographic romances that

26. Elaine Freedgood, *The Ideas in Things: Fugitive Meaning in the Victorian Novel* (Chicago: University of Chicago Press, 2006).
27. Herman Melville, *Typee* (1846; repr., New York: Penguin, 1996), 21.

describe a way of life in their own language, providing not so much thick description as thick denotation that becomes a kind of scrim of interesting words, words that resonate because we read them over and over again in what Margaret Cohen calls the "maritime book"—the massive discourse of the sea of which the novels we tend to read are but a slender slice.[28]

The discourse of which this fiction is a part is a round robin of certain generic conventions, as Rozwadowski and Cohen both show, circulated from whalers to novelists to scientists to explorers in recursive patterns; Melville borrowed from the history of the historical Mocha Dick who was finally killed in 1859 with nineteen old harpoons buried in his body, and the late Victorian naturalist Henry Moseley relied on both Darwin and Defoe for his narrative and descriptive practices. The characters in sea fiction also read the discourse of the sea. Jim, of *Lord Jim*,

> [s]aw himself saving people from sinking ships, cutting away masts in a hurricane, swimming through a surf with a line; or as a lonely castaway, barefooted and half naked, walking on uncovered reefs in search of shellfish to stave off starvation. He confronted savages on tropical shores, quelled mutinies on the high seas, and in a small boat upon the ocean kept up the hearts of despairing men—always an example of devotion to duty, and as unflinching as a hero in a book.[29]

And yet, as we know, at the crucial moment, Jim jumps ship and leaves nine hundred pilgrims to drown. Conrad promises us that if we have occasion to bring together what we imagine when we read and the actual referents that are readily available at our local ports and harbors, we too may well flinch, and jump. The pleasure of the sea novel lies, in part, in our relation to its offshore-ness: we don't have to have Jim's experience; we can just wonder about ourselves instead: would we jump too? We are

---

28. Cohen, "Traveling Genres," 485.
29. Joseph Conrad, *Lord Jim* (London: Penguin, 2000), 47.

too ironic to imagine ourselves as unflinching heroes, probably, but we may not want to decide exactly who we would be at sea.

The ballastic also describes a research problem: the problem of trying to recover undocumented material and its observable, but also still largely unrecorded, effects. Ballast is mentioned incidentally, accidentally, usually when it comes into focus as something else: as furniture, scrimshaw, or money. There had to be ballast on Conrad's imagined ships, on Melville's, on Marryat's: I imagine that it was thought of by these mariner/authors as the other details of marine engineering are so precisely rendered. But Melville mentions "ballast-stones" in passing and otherwise uses the term metaphorically—he describes Ahab's hands as ballast-like; Conrad describes shoveling sand ballast into the hold of the ship in *Youth*; Marryat has Peter Simple load it, but doesn't describe what it is. It is not of interest. This ballastic research problem might be described as a weighty absence. Ballast is a material without qualities, but not without consequences, as many confused archaeologists, numerous mahogany tables, and destroyed ecosystems testify. Ballast suggests a serious problem of record keeping and of history: we might now be failing to specify something in our own records that will have momentous effects in the future, but that at the moment has for us no need to be divided or unmoored from its generic plurality. This unrecorded but weighty matter is probably some group of things—living or not—that are as yet invisible, material lurking in an abstract noun, like the all-purpose noun and adjective "material."

Another use of "ballastic" would apply to all things that are circulated accidentally: people, plants, ideas, pots, songs, riddles, and salamanders. All the fictional characters who wind up on beaches and islands in unplanned layovers—Robinson Crusoe, Lord Jim, the beachcombers of Robert Louis Stevenson's South Seas tales, to mention some of the most famous cases—could be described as ballastic. In this sense, the ballastic is like cosmopolitanism and records, more precisely than the more usual term, the violence of circulation and worldliness, the damage that matter, ideas, and people can inflict as they circulate, carrying with them microorganisms, munitions, religions, and political economies from afar. The ballastic is also always already: before the ship arrived on the pristine island, a log or a barrel separated from a raft, carrying the potential to wreak havoc with just the few microorganisms clinging to its bark, living in its whorls.

In a late novella of Robert Louis Stevenson, *The Ebb-Tide*, the idea of the ballastic reaches a kind of luminous allegorical clarity. The novella opens thus:

> Throughout the island world of the Pacific, scattered men of many European races and from almost every grade of society carry activity and disseminate disease. Some prosper and some vegetate. Some have mounted the steps of thrones and owned islands and navies. Others, again, must marry for a livelihood, a strapping, merry, chocolate-coloured dame supports them in sheer idleness, and dressed like natives, but still retaining some foreign element of gait or attitude, still perhaps with some relic of the officer and gentleman, they sprawl in palm-leaf verandahs and entertain an island audience with memories of the music hall.[30]

We can hear in these few sentences both the historical accounts of the incursions of Westerners in the Pacific, and typical literary accounts of it as well. In *The Ebb-Tide*, an American and two Britons take over a ship with a cargo of champagne after the original crew has died of yellow fever. They decide to steal the ship and its cargo and sell them both in Peru. They begin to drink the champagne, and the captain and second mate are soon drunk around the clock. The first mate, an Oxford man down on his luck called Herrick, and the native Christian cannibal

---

30. Robert Louis Stevenson, *Treasure Island and The Ebb-Tide* (New York: Penguin, 2012), 1.

crew, remain faithful to their duties. Soon enough, the second mate, Huish, opens a bottle that doesn't pop, and the unfortunate thieves find out that after a few bottles of the good stuff on top, the rest of the putative champagne is water. The scammers have been scammed. As the captain puts it, "There's only one thing certain: there's no use carting this old glass and ballast to Peru."[31] They make landfall on another island, inhabited by a crazed missionary whom they plan to kill, but who outsmarts them. Huish is killed, the captain becomes born again, and in the last line of the novel we find him encouraging Herrick to find Christ.

The novella is widely understood to be a critique of imperialism and of the Western plunder and desecration of the Pacific. *The Ebb-Tide* illustrates the ballastic in its dark sense: in the opening of the novella, Stevenson describes the "scattering" of Europeans, and their random unloading of both activity and disease across the Pacific islands.[32] The island the three miscreants happen upon is uncharted: they just get lucky. In the Pacific, you may become a king or a vegetable or a kind of concubine depending on where you wash up and the quality of your synergy with the local population. Stevenson cites and satirizes a kind of rogue cosmopolitanism—a too-mobile population of Europeans washing up on beaches and creating biological and cultural havoc, bringing smallpox and the music hall to people who would be much better off without either. In this fantasy, native populations of the Pacific are Edenic; Stevenson would have their purity preserved for Europeans like himself, I suppose, who can appreciate it and, presumably, interact with it harmlessly. In this fantasy of authenticity, there is an idea of a world in which no mixing or miscegenation has happened and in which you, the writer, the critic, and the Victorian or Victorianist can land and bring no microorganisms or microbad attitudes along.

31. Ibid.
32. Ibid.

The idea of the ballastic scuttles this idea: there is always a cargo that is unaccounted for, undocumented and unspecified, that is reacting and interacting with the text, the island, the world you engage. Champagne can "become" ballast; ballast can become fine mahogany furniture and shell currency. It is, perhaps, radical rubbish, in Michael Thompson's idea of it: stuff that can have its value suddenly refigured, but not given time, as in Thompson's formulation, but given a form of unbounded space.[33] A cowry shell in the Maldives is a seashell, but in West Africa, even in some locations down to the present, it is currency. Ballast has another important quality: it literally cannot be decontextualized or divested of its origins and its travels: biologically, archaeologically, demographically, and culturally, the stuff that gets dumped on beaches and in harbors is not only itself an agent of change, but it is full of all kinds of small life forms that may be all too content in their new habitat. Ballast gives the lie to the notion of traveling light and even perhaps to the possibility of some primary indigeneity, or at least an indigeneity that can be known now. It reminds us of the extent to which we change, because of the things we need to carry, the texts, places, and peoples we visit. And ballast is a metaphor because it can remind us of a kind of record keeping, in fiction and in fact, that keeps a referent at bay—offshore, in an aura of denotation that remains unread.

33. Michael Thompson, *The Creation and Destruction of Value* (1979; repr., London: Pluto Press, 2017).

Omniscience

ELIZABETH GASKELL'S 1848 novel *Mary Barton* is full of poetry, but not where the characters can see it. In the epigraphs and footnotes, for the eyes of readers and narrators only, Samuel Coleridge's "Christabel," John Keats's "Hyperion," Edmund Spenser's *The Faerie Queen*, Dante's *The Divine Comedy*, John Donne's "Second Anniversary," Robert Burns's "Mary Morison," Walter Savage Landor's "The Mermaid," Tennyson's "Mariana" (which Gaskell misquotes), bits of Geoffrey Chaucer, John Wycliffe, Ben Jonson, Shakespeare, and Thomas Carlyle—all mark out the common culture of the readers of this novel, who are not the same as its characters. The epigraphs were added at the suggestion of Gaskell's publisher, Chapman and Hall, for reasons I will discuss below, and the footnotes were written by her husband, Peter Gaskell, and are "translations" of Manchester dialect that often use medieval and early modern literary sources as examples.

The reading that the characters do, or the textual matter that they hear (literacy being a complicated matter) is represented in a handful of documents, including a Manchester song, "The Oldham Weaver," which the seamstress Margaret Jennings sings and the lyrics of which the narrator transcribes for us—except that she leaves out one problematic stanza in which conflict emerges between weaver and master, thus softening the song's "note of rebelliousness";[1] the People's Charter, which Parliament refuses to read but of which the Chartist characters in the novel have probably read, or heard, a significant part; "an old *Northern Star*," a Chartist newspaper the narrator tells us John Barton has "borrowed from a neighbouring public-house,"[2] a typical source of periodicals for the poor in the period; the Bible; and a poem by Samuel Bamford, "the working class radical,"[3] that Job Legh, Margaret's autodidactic grandfather, recites and that Mary Barton then copies down, at her father's request. The apparent homogeneity of this list—all of the reading by the poor seems to concern the poor—is deceptive and relies on the middle-class reader, from 1848 to the present, having very little idea of the complexity of Chartism as a political movement with its own distinctive print culture and of the variety and cosmopolitanism of a radical paper like the *Northern Star*.

Mary copies the Bamford poem onto the blank part of a valentine sent to her by Jem Wilson in a typical nineteenth-century reuse of paper. John Barton will use half of this valentine as wadding for the gun he uses to kill Harry Carson—the son of the mill owner for whom he works—and Jem Wilson, Mary's sometime lover and future husband, will be arrested for the murder. Even the (apparently) limited reading material of the poor leads them astray. The Chartist newspaper, the (redacted) sentimental song, the sympathetic poem, the material on which it is written, and the problem of litter as a findable kind of evidence suggest that reading and writing are activities that require careful guidance— the kind a narrator can provide in some case, a philosopher in

---

1. C. M. Jackson-Houlston, *Ballads, Songs, and Snatches: The Appropriation of Folk Song and Popular Culture in British Nineteenth-Century Realist Prose* (Aldershot: Ashgate, 1999), 108.

2. Elizabeth Gaskell, *Mary Barton* (New York: Penguin, 1996), 82.

3. Martin Hewitt, "Radicalism and the Working Class: The Case of Samuel Bamford," *Historical Journal* 34, no. 4 (1991): 873.

others, in the arguments of Jacques Rancière.[4] The poor of the novelist, I will argue, are both the literally and subjectively poor characters of *Mary Barton*—fictional characters in the history of the novel more generally who must, for generic logistical reasons, be subjectively poorer than their narrators—and readers, who require all kinds of narrators, in the novel and outside it, to help them (us) navigate the world and its texts. The "poor" of the novelist are physically, materially, intellectually, and emotionally less than their narrators, and their poverty limits their experiences in ways that fictions of certain kinds have rendered as a kind of metalepsis, in which a narrator and characters are in different worlds in a social, rather than an existential, sense. This case study considers the industrial poor of nineteenth-century Britain and alludes to other kinds of poverty in later novels about other kinds of "poor" characters, characters who suffer from or evade the pyschic and textual rupture of omniscience, and its key technique: free indirect discourse.

Inventing a Culture for the Poor

John Barton kills Harry Carson, the mill owner's son, because during a meeting of masters and men, Harry draws caricatures of the men, which he carelessly throws at the fire but which are not burned. The laboring men pick up the drawings (they think their children will enjoy them) and are deeply hurt by the pictures—they recognize themselves immediately in the sad details of their ragged clothing. They declare that they could take a joke as well as the next person if they and their families were not starving, or as Manchester dialect has it,

4. See Jacques Rancière, "The Putting to Death of Emma Bovary: Literature, Democracy and Medicine," in *The Politics of Literature*, trans. Julie Rose (Cambridge: Polity Press, 2011), 49–71; and *The Philosopher and His Poor*, trans. John Drury, Corinne Oster, and Andrew Parker (Durham, NC: Duke University Press, 2004).

"clemming"—a frequent topic in the novel. Starving men, the novel tells us, cannot abide satire. Not because they cannot understand it but because they are in too much pain to laugh at themselves. And in fact the details are painfully unfunny: "that's me, by G_d," an anonymous mill worker exclaims; "it's the very way I'm obligated to pin my waistcoat up, to hide that I've getten no shirt. That is a shame, and I'll not stand it."[5] The poor, this scene suggests, require a kind of literal and respectful realism. Thus the reading of this novel's characters itemized above: an apparently simple diet of items that are immediately for and about them.

An even more constrictive subjective effect of poverty is constructed by Gaskell in her imagining of John Barton's pilgrimage to London to present the People's Charter to Parliament. Barton is represented during his trip to London as an uncomprehending noncitizen of modernity: he thinks naked statues are signs for tailors' shops and all carriages with feathers are hearses (as Methodist hearses were so styled). "I were like a child," he says, and so we as readers think too: he is literal minded and incapable of what one might call interpretation or figuration.[6] Everything is based very strictly on his own experience; he cannot imagine the idea of an ornamental statue or a decorated carriage—even though the novel is regularly punctuated with painful encounters of starving workers watching the wives of mill owners coming out of shops laden with purchases, often getting into what must be similar carriages. Still, Barton cannot partake of even the most concrete items of what Rancière calls the "common culture."[7]

The title of the Bamford poem that Mary copies between the lines of the valentine is not titled in the novel, but is called "God Help the Poor," and that phrase is repeated in the first and last

5. Gaskell, *Mary Barton*, 187.
6. Ibid., 101.
7. Rancière, *The Politics of Literature*, 173.

lines of all five stanzas, and "God help" is repeated many times in between. Poverty is described realistically in the poem but in a grammar more affecting than the prose of *Mary Barton* and in a regular rhyme scheme, which also makes it more mentally portable, because more readily memorizable, than any prose could be. The poem also explores the experience of cold and hunger repeatedly:

> God help the poor! Behold you famished lad,
> No shoes, nor hose, his wounded feet protect;
> With limping gait, and looks so dreamy sad,
> He wanders onward, stopping to inspect
> Each window, stored with articles of food.[8]

The lad is not simply a barefoot boy—he has been abandoned by both shoes and socks—he is doubly deprived of the two things that might protect his feet, which are wounded like those of Christ. And indeed shoes and hose are the subject of the clause— his feet the passive, helpless, damaged object. He limps because of these wounds, and possibly others, and looks at food in shop windows, which is lavishly and, for the famished lad, cruelly displayed behind the newly mass-produced plate glass windows that changed shops and shopping in the mid-nineteenth century. His "sad"-ness is a weak rhyme for the "food" that he will not eat. His condition could, of course, be readily improved by someone other than God. Bandages, hose, shoes, and food would help him enormously.

The characters empathizing with the famished lad can do very little to alleviate the misery of those like him. The novel shows them doing whatever they can for their own starving friends and neighbors, pawning their very small "superfluities" in order to buy food and coal, but the mill owners, who might provide substantial help, refuse responsibility for the suffering of their workers, insisting that workers, along with everyone else,

8. Gaskell, *Mary Barton*, 158.

accept market downturns. "It [the demand for labor] depends on events which God alone can control," as John Carson, the mill owner, puts it.[9] The poem inside the novel suggests to middle-class readers that they ought to be moved, as the poor are moved, by simple descriptions of poverty: the middle class is immersed in the "culture" of the poor that the novel invents. It also suggests that the poor are limited in their intellectual pursuits by their immiseration: they do not, in the confines of this novel, read material that does not concern their immediate needs and problems.

If, as Rancière argues in *The Philosopher and His Poor*, for Plato, Karl Marx, Jean-Paul Sartre, and Pierre Bourdieu the poor are consumed by poverty and cannot think beyond it,[10] in this novel of poverty, the *reader* cannot do anything other than be consumed by the idea that poverty is subjectively crushing; Sartre's description of the function of exhaustion seems ineluctable: "At first sight there is not in principle the least difficulty in an unskilled worker's making an excellent militant: the only serious obstacle would seem vulgar and circumstantial: it is fatigue. Only there it is: this fatigue is not an accident; it accumulates without melting, like the eternal snows, and it *makes* the unskilled workers."[11] A novel like *Mary Barton* convinces us of this apparent truth once again. This is perhaps why Chapman and Hall, Gaskell's publisher, insisted that she add the epigraphs: to keep the two nations literally on the page, in their separate textual spaces, although if we follow the recent work of Mike Sanders and Greg Vargo, among others, on the Chartist press, we know that its pages were full of the literature Gaskell cites—not yet canonical or high brow in historical terms, but seeming in Gaskell's account to belong to those who are not the laboring poor.

9. Gaskell, *Mary Barton*, 384.
10. Ranciére, *The Philosopher and His Poor*.
11. Jean-Paul Sartre, *The Communists and Peace, with a Reply to Claude Lefort* (New York: George Brazillier, 1968), 212.

Two Nations, Two Cultures

Again and again over the past sixty or so years, scholars have had to assert and reassert laboring class traditions of autodidacticism; students of the radical press must produce evidence of the reprinting of Milton, Southey, Byron, Shelley, Wordsworth, and Dickens in various papers and pamphlets as evidence of the intellectual life of that class. "[L]iterary historians," Greg Vargo argues, "have too readily accepted middle-class writers' descriptions of the gulf separating 'the two nations,'" in which the middle class was isolated from the radical press and the working class was isolated from the "polite" press. "The cultural reality of social division was different, characterized on both sides by argument, contest, parody, and appropriation rather than by separation and ignorance."[12] Mike Sanders argues that "with determination and a degree of good fortune, the [laboring class] autodidact could complete a course of reading which would stand comparison with many a contemporary undergraduate syllabus."[13] Chartists, for example, were active educators, poets, and publishers. Ian Haywood suggests that Chartists believed that "in order to prove themselves worthy of political representation, it was a vital task to conquer the realm of symbolic representation."[14] In this they were well attuned to the liberal cultural critics of the mid-century, including George Eliot,

12. Greg Vargo, *An Underground History of Early Victorian Fiction: Chartism, Radical Print Culture, and the Social Problem Novel* (Cambridge: Cambridge University Press, 2018), 8.

13. Mike Sanders, *The Poetry of Chartism: Aesthetics, Politics and History* (Cambridge: Cambridge University Press, 2009), 8. See also Martha Vicinus, *The Industrial Muse: A Study of Nineteenth-Century British Working Class Literature* (New York: Barnes and Noble, 1975); David Vincent, *Bread, Knowledge and Freedom: A Study of Nineteenth-Century Working Class Autobiography* (New York: Routledge, 1982); and Jonathan Rose, *The Intellectual Life of the Nineteenth-Century Working Class* (New Haven, CT: Yale University Press, 2001).

14. Ian Haywood, *The Literature of Chartist Struggle: An Anthology of Chartist Fiction* (Aldershot: Scholar Press, 1995), ix.

who, as Catherine Gallagher has argued, firmly believed that the representation of the laboring class ought to occur in the novel and not in the state: like Matthew Arnold, she worried that they could not see beyond the interests of "their own order."[15]

The subjectively and physically impoverished fictional population of Gaskell's "Tale of Manchester Life" is in conversation with what Haywood describes as the proliferating "didactic and agitational fiction in both radical and polite periodicals [which] constituted a highly politicised literary subculture."[16] Industrial novels like *Mary Barton* were influenced by the fiction published in the radical press and, in part, tried to answer or modify its arguments. Vargo argues that fiction like Gaskell's was profoundly influenced by Chartist fiction in particular and that this "secret history" of the mid-Victorian novel needs to be understood, as does its occlusion, as an effacement of the agency and influence of Chartist cultural energy.[17]

Gaskell knew many Manchester mill workers in her capacity as a minister's wife in that city. She also knew the autodidact and prolific writer Bamford quite well and thus had an example of the kind of laboring-class person whose reading was quite similar to her own and who exemplifies the autodidact tradition studied by Martha Vicinus, Mike Sanders, David Vincent, and Jonathan Rose, among others.[18] Bamford was a great reader and reciter of Tennyson and through Gaskell's intervention received a signed copy of Tennyson's works for his seventieth birthday. In the note he writes to thank Tennyson, he says that Tennyson's language "is almost unlimitedly expressive. This language of ours [he continues], what can it not be made to say? What height, what depth filled with all glorious hues, terrible glooms,

15. Qtd. in Catherine Gallagher, *The Industrial Reformation of English Fiction: Social Discourse and Narrative Form, 1832–1867* (Chicago: University of Chicago Press, 1985), 224.

16. Ian Haywood, *Revolution in Popular Literature: Print, Politics, and the People 1790–1860* (Cambridge: Cambridge University Press, 2009), 141.

17. Vargo, *An Underground History of Early Victorian Fiction.*

18. Sanders, *The Poetry of Chartism.*

and vivid flashes does it not combine and your poems exhibit all?"[19] "This language of *ours*," Bamford writes, claiming a common tongue with Tennyson.[20] Indeed, Gaskell is having her characters speak a dialect that she frequently footnotes for clarification, as if she and they and we were not speaking a common language at all, and yet the examples used (by Peter Gaskell) are from the works of a "great" English lineage, including Chaucer, Wycliffe, Spenser, Jonson, Shakespeare, and Skelton, suggesting that it is the middle class who may not be speaking the finest—or what Gaskell might have thought of as the most expressive—English. Gordon Bigelow argues that "the text makes an argument that the poor remain closer to an original English linguistic heritage, while a more mobile middle class becomes increasingly distant from it."[21] It is undergoing, as the language of the professionals at Jem's trial suggests, "a pitiless standardization."[22] Gaskell thus creates a portrait, a culture, and a set of characters that cannot seem to settle down entirely into the world she creates. Indeed, two worlds seem to come in and out of focus: a robust, working-class culture with strong regional and historical linguistic usages, profound political affiliations, and extraordinary personal loyalty. In another world that frequently eclipses this one, the poor can only be poor.

John Barton may like Bamford's poem, but it is doubtful that an actual Chartist would have wanted a copy of it. Bamford was a radical only through the Peterloo riot and massacre—that is, up to the 1820s. He becomes an opponent of Chartism in the 1830s, at one point becoming a constable in order to help put down a demonstration.[23] He also becomes a writer of poetry for several middle-class newspapers in London rather than for any

19. Qtd. in Hallam Lord Tennyson, *Alfred Lord Tennyson: A Memoir by His Son* (New York: Macmillan and Co., 1897), 286.

20. Ibid.

21. Gordon Bigelow, *Fiction, Famine, and the Rise of Economics in Victorian Britain and Ireland* (Cambridge: Cambridge University Press, 2003), 148.

22. Ibid., 149.

23. Hewitt, "Radicalism and the Working Class," 873.

of the many radical papers being published in the period. His poetry bewails the condition of the poor, but it does so without offering a political program to remedy it. Gaskell gives her radical characters a radical poet who no longer is one; she represents as radical poetry that has become as sentimental, and essentially aristocratic, as her own ideas about easing the suffering of the laboring class.

Letters and Litter

Mary Barton's plot turns on the dangerous instability and circulation of refunctioned paper, a kind of literalization of Rancière's "errant letter," the emblem of the literary in his thinking, but rehabilitated: In the eighteenth and nineteenth centuries, the audience for writing is no longer "a relationship of address regulated between speech acts and defined audiences." It is the

> new regime of the art of writing in which the writer is anyone at all and the reader is anyone at all. In this respect, the sentences of novelists could be compared to mute stones. They were mute in the sense in which Plato had opposed the "mute paintings" of writing to the living words of speech dropped by the master like so many seeds destined to grow in the soul of the disciple. Literature is the reign of writing, of speech circulating outside any determined relationship of address. . . . [I]t circulates . . . without a master to accompany it.[24]

The valentine/poem/wadding has three "writers": Jem as valentine writer and Bamford the poet via Mary as transcriber, and it has for its random readers Mary, John Barton, Esther, and then Mary again. The wadding similarly circulates randomly as a poem in John Barton's pocket, as mere paper that comes to hand to fill a gun, and then as waste paper that catches the observant eye of Mary's Aunt Esther, who is trained to see well at

24. Ranciére, *The Politics of Literature*, 12.

night by her career as a prostitute and who brings it to Mary—to keep the secret and destroy it at the same time. We have here the kind of chronic Victorian miniature archival crisis described by Priyanka Anne Jacob, in which both saving and throwing away various kinds of text might prove disastrous and in whose history the pigeonhole, the memo, the filing cabinet, the paper shredder, and the forensic and hygienic problems of litter have all had consequential roles.[25] The vicissitudes of rubbish versus text are difficult to predict as a piece of paper moves among various writers, readers, hands, pockets, streets, and courts. These errant letters lose their way, they lose their authors, and they lose their connection to the authors of the crime with which they are associated. The letters cross paths with the character in the novel, drawing the lines of the plot as they go. They also "cross" the text with the ghostly presence of other texts: internal paratexts of a kind, sometimes not, as in the case of the Bamford poem, to be written by Gaskell herself. They are quotations of the kind that litter the footnotes.

Gaskell waxes Platonic in her concern for the fate of human characters caught up in the agency of the typographic characters that circulate among them, between them, and around them, creating circumstances that only the novelist can finally organize or undo: no reading, no interpretation—by characters or extradiegetic readers—can put the valentine back in the right pocket or the gun in the right hand. We are all—fictional characters and actual persons—dependent on our author and narrator to explain the speech, and the feeling, behind the letters and their various destinations. We all need someone to talk to rather than something to read. And the narrator is the "function" of the novel that speaks to readers, the one whose adumbration of the speech of others must be trusted—or not. This diffusion of the difference between

25. Priyanka Anne Jacob, "The Relic and the Ruin: Equivocal Objects and the Presence of the Past in *Daniel Deronda*," *Victorian Literature and Culture* 44, no. 4 (2016): 333–57.

diegetic layers suggests an implosive metalepsis, in which the real and fictional reciprocally burst each other's boundaries, a "world" that is not realistic in a literary sense.

Rancière's democratic vision of the literary relies on the idea of the errant letter: the novel is the text that is written for no particular audience; it can go anywhere and be read by anyone. This is not quite true of a novel like *Mary Barton*, which was published in two expensive volumes by Chapman and Hall and would have been, like most Victorian novels, beyond the reach of the poor represented in it. What the Bartons and the Wilsons could have afforded to read would have been cheap versions of out-of-copyright eighteenth-century novels, penny dreadfuls, pamphlets, broadsides, and the productions of the radical press. So the errancy of the letter is practically and economically circumscribed. Novelists at this juncture in the nineteenth century had some knowledge of who was going to read their work. This is why Gaskell can represent John Barton's protosocialist theory of value uncontested by a more laissez-faire account of value, and why she can represent Chartism, strikes, trade unions, and the murder of a master. Indeed, Gaskell, if she were worried about the fullness (representativeness) of her contemporary audience, might not have written this novel at all.

The Democratic Novel and Democratic Narration

In his introduction to *The Philosopher and His Poor*, Andrew Parker describes Rancière's project as asking if "philosophy [can] ever refrain from thinking for" the poor.[26] If we ask the same question about the novelist, the answer is obviously and obdurately no: the job of the novelist is to invent characters and thus their thoughts and then to narrate them through direct and indirect discourse. In the preface to *Mary Barton*, Gaskell

26. Parker, introduction to Rancière, *The Philosopher and His Poor*, ix.

describes her subjects: "The more I reflected on this unhappy state of things between those so bound to each other by common interests, as the employers and the employed must ever be, the more anxious I became to give some utterance to the agony which, from time to time, convulses this dumb people."[27] In this same preface, Gaskell insists that she is not writing a novel of "Political Economy or the theories of trade";[28] her decision about the "dumbness" of the Manchester "employed" is an eminently political decision, in Rancière's definition: "[A]ll political activity is a conflict aimed at deciding what is speech or mere growl; in other words, aimed at retracing the perceptible boundaries by means of which political capacity is demonstrated."[29] Gaskell decides, before the novel begins, that her characters have no political capacity: they are growling, and she is translating. This claim is made at a moment when workers all over Britain are "speaking" massively: in demonstrations, strikes, in the "extraordinary articulate and disciplined" movement of Chartism,[30] and vividly and copiously in a wealth of radical publications that are hugely various in their content. And Gaskell *is representing all of this*, however sketchily and condescendingly in *Mary Barton*.

She is, we might say, a conflicted capitalist. Sometimes the growl comes out in a language, as I have discussed above, that is more moving, more true to Gaskell's idea of the poetic properties of English than anything she can give us in her own, standardized language. She gives to John Barton a coherent understanding of the labor theory of value, even if it is a version of it with which she would disagree, and she gives it to us in all the luster of Manchester English:

27. Gaskell, *Mary Barton*, 3.

28. Ibid., 4.

29. Rancière, *The Politics of Literature*, 4.

30. Dorothy Thompson points out that British workers "responded to hunger by forming a nation-wide movement around a political programme instead of by more traditional means of protest like food rioting, arson, begging, poaching, or praying" (Dorothy Thompson, introduction to *The Early Chartists* [London: Palgrave Macmillan, 1971], 12).

> You'll say (at least many a one does), they'n getten capital
> an'we'n getten none, I say, our labour's our capital, and we
> ought to draw interest on that. They get interest on their cap-
> ital somehow a' this time, while ourn is lying idle, else how
> could they live as they do? Besides, there's many on'em has
> had nought to begin wi'; there's Carsons, and Duncombes,
> and Mengies, and many another, as comed into Manchester
> with clothes to their back, and that were all, and now they're
> worth their tens of thousands, a'getten out of our labour. . . .
> They'n screwed us down to th'lowest peg, in order to make
> their great big fortunes, and build their great big houses, and
> we, why we're just clemming, many and many of us.[31]

This language is not difficult to read, but it is different, obviously, from that of the narrator. Its "ourn's" are mournful, the
repetition of "many and many" is melodic and balefully copious,
and the abbreviated articles and propositions suggest a way of
talking that cannot luxuriate over consonants that can be understood without being sounded.

Barton makes this speech to his friend George Wilson, who
has no argument to refute it except that he believes that "th'
masters suffer too" in bad times.[32] The answer, the solution,
lies with the reader—the middle-class reader—who is enjoined
by the text to both alleviate (with alms and sympathy rather
than better wages) the suffering of the poor and to display *their
own* suffering during hard times. Still, Gaskell gives Barton a
moment of strong and eloquent articulation, even if the thrust
of the novel is that Barton misunderstands the fact that capi-
talists do actually risk and sometimes lose everything—in their
capital if not in their bodies, to paraphrase Marx. Gaskell gives
us a strong illustration of a political movement: she opens the
novel to dissensus, to the coexistence of two worlds, even if she
will not pursue "a possible world in which the argument [the

31. Gaskell, *Mary Barton*, 104.
32. Ibid., 105.

Chartist argument in this case] could count as an argument . . .
a paradoxical world that puts together two separate worlds."[33]
The two worlds remain, jostling one another, asking us to make
sense of them or to accept that multiple worlds, like multiple
nations, can simply coexist if we can hold them firmly in mind.

The novel cannot resolve these two worlds into one because it
is British, reformist, and ultimately aristocratic and not French,
realistic, and democratic. In the democratic novel as it is developed by Honoré de Balzac and Gustave Flaubert, Rancière
argues, every object, situation, and person is equal: action has
been overtaken by things; events by everyday life. Art is style; its
content is negligible. A curiosity shop can be a poem, as it is in
Balzac's *La peau de chagrin*. Rancière notes,

> In this shop, objects of all ages and from all civilizations are
> jumbled together. But, so, too, art objects and religious and
> luxury objects are jumbled together with objects from ordi-
> nary life: stuffed crocodiles, monkeys or boas seem to smile
> at church windows or to want to bite various busts. A Sèvres
> vase rubs shoulders with an Egyptian sphinx, Madame Du
> Barry gazes at an Indian pipe, and a pneumatic tube pokes
> the emperor Augustus in the eye. This shop where every-
> thing is jumbled together composes, says Balzac, an endless
> poem. The poem is double: it is the poem of the great equal-
> ity of things noble and vile, ancient and modern, decorative
> and utilitarian. But it is also, conversely, the deployment of
> objects that are all also and at the same time fossils of an age,
> hieroglyphics of a civilization.[34]

Sèvres vases, sphinxes, and pneumatic tubes are all part of the
known bourgeois world: readers can interpret these objects without commentary from the narrator. In *Mary Barton*, the object

33. Jacques Rancière, *Dissensus: On Politics and Aesthetics*, trans. Steven
Corcoran (London: Continuum, 2010), 39.

34. Rancière, *The Politics of Literature*, 15.

world is exotic and requires too much explanation to become the kind of obvious archaeological evidence that it provides in Balzac. John Barton's silk scarf is an investment that must be explained as such: it is an item bought in good times that can be pawned in bad in order to feed a starving neighbor; a geranium on a window sill is not a random houseplant but a deep signifier of a laboring-class domesticity (and its accompanying protection of the private sphere from the public by way of foliage) of which middle-class readers may be entirely unaware. The objects in this landscape are subjects that must be given a discourse by the narrator. They are not ready, in literary or historical terms, for objectification.

Gaskell's unnamed narrator is a first-person narrator who is not officially a character[35] and in fact gives every impression of being the author—the same "I" of the preface seems to be the "I" who narrates. The effect of this is that the novel takes place in a kind of twilight zone of authorial creation/observation. But the narrator, because she is officially intradiegetic, can engage only gingerly in one of the most important formal devices of the novel: free indirect discourse. Jem Wilson's thoughts, for example, are articulated in free indirect discourse for two brief sentences and then revert to indirect discourse: "Mary loved another! Oh! How should he bear it?"[36]

The subjectivity of the poor, perhaps, does not need this narration: the language of mill and millinery workers can be adequately represented by the friend of the poor who thinks for them and who can adequately represent them from the "outside." But perhaps they simply do not read enough to have the kinds of thoughts that narrators engaging in free indirect discourse so often like to quote—the flotsam and jetsam of bad novels in the case of Emma Bovary and Catherine Morland; Casaubon's

35. That is to say, a first-person narrator like Pip or Jane Eyre can ventriloquize their younger selves, but Gaskell's narrator offers no self, younger or current, to thus narrate.

36. Gaskell, *Mary Barton*, 165. Thanks to Cannon Schmitt for pointing out this instance of free indirect discourse.

bad philology; Dombey's bad business. Gaskell surrounds her characters with literary allusions, but they belong to the narrator: they are not the stuff of a character's thoughts. Occasionally a biblical quotation or a line from Robert Burns emerges as the thought of a character, but in general, the recycled verbiage that makes up free indirect discourse is not part of the subjective world of the characters.

Moreover, *Mary Barton*'s narrator is not removed from the action. The narrator of *Madame Bovary* is nothing like Madame Bovary and has no sympathy for her. Emma Bovary is "[t]he sentimental person [who] requires the ideal pleasures of literature and art to be concrete pleasures."[37] The narrator is an objective artist. Emma Bovary must die so that the narrator can live, having rid himself of the build-up of her kitsch, which would destroy his soul if he could not actively disavow it by killing her off. Gaskell's narrator seems to be the very "I" of the preface; that is, she seems to be Elizabeth Gaskell herself. Not only is she not removed from the action, but she seems to be recording action and creating a novel by turns. But like Flaubert's narrator, Gaskell, our author and narrator, also kills a character. John Barton must die because he requires that his political actions result in concrete political changes. With the failure of the People's Charter, he becomes a trade unionist.[38] He only becomes open to the narrator's solution, which is to accept and be comforted by the milk of the master's kindness, on his deathbed—and in fact he dies in John Carson's (the mill owner's) forgiving arms, his trade unionism extinguished at every level.

Gaskell's novel reduces politics to feeling; it removes the laboring-class characters from the public sphere in which they are seeking to represent themselves and returns them to,

37. Rancière, *Politics of Literature*, 51.

38. Patrick Brantlinger argues that "[w]hereas Mrs. Gaskell presents Barton's Chartism sympathetically," she identifies his trade unionism with his turn to violence ("The Case against Trade Unions in Early Victorian Fiction," *Victorian Studies* 13, no. 1 [1969]: 37).

or attempts to return them to—in what will, hopefully, be the "sequel" to the novel—private, affective relationships with each other and with their employers. The ultimate solution of *Mary Barton*, Gaskell's Unitarian liberal solution, is charity, which is why her novel is ultimately aristocratic, and why there inheres in liberalism, until at least the end of the nineteenth century, a strong strain of noblesse oblige.[39] *Mary Barton* is a melodrama and not a realist novel, and it is profoundly not the democratic novel described by Rancière in his analysis of Balzac and Flaubert, writers who are not prescribing reforms but working out styles of realistic representation.

And this rescues *Mary Barton*'s characters as subjects, in one of the strangest of literary historical turns: it is in this deeply un-"psychological" novel that characters get to have subjectivities; they wish to represent *themselves*, and the author ultimately, unwittingly, colludes with her characters in that wish. Emma Bovary's "interior self" is made up of the litter of the romances she reads, and the narrator's ventriloquizing of this language shames her—for her excessive purchases, for her ideas of romance, for her tacky suicide. Free indirect discourse of this kind humiliates characters and gives readers a kind of frisson and a kind of fright, because the thoughts any of us might think and not speak are very often thoughts that are less original, acute, smart, ironic, and knowing than those of a narrator who can invent, narrate, ironize, and refine them. In fact, many of us may go around with only very partially modified "lines" from various grubby sources floating around in our silent narratives of ourselves—lines we are glad there is no narrator around to cast in the kind of squirm-inducing display that free indirect discourse can create. Indeed, perhaps free indirect discourse is not so much a representation of subjectivity as a representation

39. See Lauren Goodlad, "'Making the Working Man Like Me': Charity, Pastorship, and Middle-Class Identity in Nineteenth-Century Britain; Thomas Chalmers and Dr. James Philips Kay," *Victorian Studies* 43, no. 4 (2001): 591–617.

of the intertextuality of representations of subjectivity, including those we make to ourselves about ourselves. Not so much telepathy, omniscience, or an ultimate instance of the police, free indirect discourse is a kind of satire of the way in which we all recycle language—and is itself another kind of recycling. It is a poem written over a valentine turned into the wadding for a gun that might kill someone. Or cause an author to have to kill a character.

Free indirect discourse makes characters poor so that narrators can remain rich: narrators are after all in control of the means of production of this kind of subjectivity effect, and the character cannot be greater than its narrator. In the case of fiction, the idea of the writer/narrator as capitalist seems pretty fair, since the labor of the character is, after all, accomplished by the author/narrator. But at the moment of free indirect discourse, the narrator splits away from that creation, giving us the characters we think of as people—even though they are made up of textual bits and pieces that the narrator knits into sentences— the ones with whom we identify, however mistakenly, however correctly. We are caught up in a metaleptic subjectivity that we can theorize—via Lacan, Althusser, Fanon, or Irigaray, to name just a few theorists of subjective fracture—but it is very hard to live this cleft ontology.

Free indirect discourse may be cruel, but, at least with respect to readers, it is democratic: it assumes an interiority that can only be narrated by a superhuman being, and it assumes that interiority is very often (in and out of fiction) a literary technique. Readers get to share the power of the narrator; they are equal, for the duration of reading, to their head of state, the ruler of the novel's world. But it is not democratic where characters are concerned, for characters are impoverished by free indirect discourse. Subjectivity is, in that mode of narration, a literary effect, sometimes literally, as when characters' thoughts are, like Emma's, bits and pieces of bad romances. Characters who are spared this invasion—like those in *Mary Barton*—remain intact as possible subjects. Their interiority is unknown, but it is not nonexistent. Gaskell's characters are poor in spirit, poor in material goods, poor in intellectual accomplishment, but they are wealthier than the average fictional character that will succeed them in that they can or could, in the hands of a different writer in a different genre or century, potentially represent themselves.

Gaskell leaves a margin of freedom in the first-person narrator that prevents free indirect discourse, and the same can be said of the linguistic rupture of the text. The language of her characters is too radically different from that of the narrator to allow the voices of characters and narrator to mingle in the nearly seamless way that free indirect discourse requires. Her characters' thoughts and feelings can be translated by a sympathetic narrator, but they are not represented from the inside. The gaps, which are maintained in the epigraphs, main text, and footnotes, are a space of freedom for the characters, who cannot, finally, be spoken for in their entirety as subjects and who therefore have yet to be represented fully in novelistic terms. In leaving open that possibility in the future, Gaskell leaves it to the laboring-class characters themselves. This may be why she removes her characters to suburban Toronto at the novel's end: the ramifications of that self-representation will be safely distant.

Coda

We might expect that essentially white-collar characters in a late twentieth-century metafiction would fare better in terms of representation than do the poor of an industrial novel by a liberal Victorian. History returns as farce in Gilbert Sorrentino's 1979 novel, *Mulligan Stew*, itself a kind of sequel to Flann O'Brien's 1939 *At-Swim-Two Birds*, in which we find a satire of the plight of a writer who "loses touch" with his characters because they literally walk off the job, hoping to be employed by better writers. Martin Halpin, a character in a novel in progress called *Red Guinea* (which is being written inside *Mulligan Stew*), by the washed-up, would-be postmodernist Antony Lamont, is out-raged to have been "plucked out of the wry, the amused footnote in which I have resided, faceless, for all these years in the work of that gentlemanly Irishman, Mr. Joyce. . . . 'An old gardener' so I've been these thirty-odd years, an old gardener who has never gardened, never even seen . . . a garden, and happy *not* to have seen one, by God!"[40] Halpin and his cocharacter Ned Beaumont, who was previously employed by Dashiell Hammett in *The Glass Key*, want to leave the Lamont novel, but they are anxious. Halpin asks, "If we should desert this novel, will we ever find employment again? . . . [W]ill the desertion be con-strued as proof of our unreliability? Authors can be strange."[41] These novelistic workers are horrified by the novel in which they find themselves—the words they have to say, the sex they have to perform, the fact that the cabin in the woods seems to have been stolen from another writer (because it is such a cliché)—a suspicion that is confirmed when mail arrives for a character in yet another novel. Quitting the novel, like the political activity in *Mary Barton*, is obviously risky. Like the advocates of the six points of the People's Charter, the characters in *Mulligan Stew* want better representation. But in this twentieth-century novel, the striking characters do not plan to represent themselves. They have no selves to represent: their only existence lies in what they have done on the page. Halpin is terrified of an upcoming res-taurant scene because he has never eaten before. These charac-ters are postpsychological; they cannot be narrated from within: they are closer to typographic than human characters. They wish to be represented, but not as themselves. They want good situa-tions, good roles, and comfortable places on the page.

Chartism was treated by the terrified middle class like a revolutionary movement precisely because of its demand that laboring class subjects be allowed to represent themselves. It

40. Gilbert Sorrentino, *Mulligan Stew* (New York: Grove Press, 1979), 25.
41. Ibid., 89.

was entirely liberal in its demands and yet entirely revolutionary because the wrong group of people was demanding that their ability to think beyond their immediate ken and outside their own rank be given the recognition of parliamentary participation, both as voters and as members. The demand for greater (larger, fuller, more accurate) representation is denied in *Mary Barton* on two fronts, that of the novel and that of the state. As Chartists well knew, and as Catherine Gallagher has argued in terms of the "industrial reformation" of the English novel, these forms of representation are deeply involved in the nineteenth century and regularly analogized to one another, perhaps most famously in Eliot's novel of the first Reform Act, *Middlemarch*.[42]

In *Mulligan Stew*, the desire for better representation (in the 1970s, it is question of lifestyle) begins to be addressed when Beaumont leaves the cabin, finds a colony of unemployed characters awaiting new authors (authorities), and finally convinces Halpin to join him. They have no agency—either their own or the employment kind through which white-collar workers in the 1970s might have sought new work. Although omniscient narration has theoretically declined by the late twentieth century—both in literary history and in this novel—these characters do not seem to have the option of becoming first-person narrators. Why not write memoirs about their lives as characters? Even in 1979, "personalities" were engaged in such projects. In this novel, and in the literary project—modern and postmodern—of which it is a part, the representation of such a self is impossible. Omniscience returns with a particular vengeance when the postpsychological novel insists on its own status and that of "everyone" in it as paper and ink.

It may be that all novels are finally omnisciently narrated— whether they are focalized, written in the first person, postmodern and dispersed, or otherwise lacking an apparent central

42. Gallagher, *The Industrial Reformation of English Fiction.*

authority. D. A. Miller makes this case about *David Copperfield* in *The Novel and the Police*: "the narrator . . . is so completely defaced that even when he becomes a name like David Copperfield, Phiz hardly knows what 'phiz' to give him."[43] The narrator always "knows" more than she tells, and the novelist, of course, knows even more than that. And our pleasure in narration requires this gappiness. "Curiosity, suspense and surprise," Meir Sternberg points out, are all driven by wanting to know more, by knowing that we do not know enough.[44] We are poor in knowledge as readers. What we always know is that there is all this stuff we do not know. We sign up for this fissured ontology and then enjoy it; it is a honeycombed knowledge we are already experienced with in other kinds of omniscience to which we also give our consent—that of our government, for example, in a state of largely silent amazement and acceptance. The pleasure of the text is also the pleasure of consenting to not knowing, to knowing that we do not know and having that be a condition of our being in the world. We do not identify with characters because they are like people, but because we are like characters, relying on forms of omniscience—governments, gravity, laws of the market, expert advice, and so on—to keep narrating various aspects of reality for us. Omniscience hangs around as an omnipresent narrative and epistemological form. Disembodied but not disempowered, dismembered but not defunctioned. You can walk out, but you cannot walk away.

The democracy of literature is always outside of it, I would argue, in acts of interpretation that link its modes of knowing and being to our own lived experience. "[I]nterpretations are themselves real changes," Rancière writes, "when they transform the forms of visibility a common world may take and, with them, the capacities that ordinary bodies may exercise in that

43. D. A. Miller, *The Novel and the Police* (Berkeley: University of California Press, 1988), 209.

44. Meir Sternberg, *The Poetics of Biblical Narrative: Ideological Literature and Drama of Reading* (Bloomington: Indiana University Press, 1985), 259.

world over a new landscape of the common."[45] They must also transform the forms of invisibility that govern our passivity, our acquiescence to all "narration" that is extradiegetic. Narration should be part of the common world; it should not only be visible but also and always audible, legible, comprehensible, and accessible. Since technology, law, and power will keep changing the meaning of all of the words just listed, the work of noticing narration requires a major humanitarian effort by the poor, a category that must always include ourselves.

45. Rancière, *Dissensus*, 30.

Paratext

THE PARATEXT IS typically considered extradiegetic, and as such it is often experienced as optional. We can say that we have read *Middlemarch* without reading every single epigraph; we can certainly ignore footnotes at will, especially if they were written by an actual editor (as opposed to the many fictional ones in Maria Edgeworth or Sir Walter Scott, which require our attention as an integral part of the text). Indeed, fictional paratexts may be more powerful than scholarly ones; autographic notes are perhaps more significant for most literary readers than are allographic additions. This chapter will consider paratexts—both epigraphs and footnotes—in *Middlemarch*, Catherine Parr Traill's *The Canadian Crusoes*, Rudyard Kipling's *Kim*, and José Rizal's *Noli Me Tangere* as a way to examine bibliographic metalepsis: the infinite library that lurks in the margins of the text, and sometimes breaks through them because of the force of an allusion, the impact of information, or the oddness of bits of text attached but also detachable from the "main" text we read.

In the texts considered in this case study, Eliot combines epigraphs written by herself and others—following the practice of both Wordsworth and Scott; Parr Traill includes authorial footnotes to explain Canadian flora and fauna to her British readers, and the *Noli* and *Kim* have been annotated more recently by scholarly editors, and include many translations into English of Tagalog, Hindi, and Urdu words. This heterogeneous grouping allows us to think about reading—the novels themselves, and the infinite library to which they gesture. Each head- and footnote asks us to consider the contours of diegetic space, and how far outside that space we must go to "read" properly, thoroughly, and knowledgeably. We perhaps enact figurally a major geographical paradox, one that will become literal in the conclusion of this study: "the ordering of space and projection of power across space is associated with the drawing of lines of movement (which can cross boundary lines) as well as the drawing of boundary lines (that purport to restrict movement)."[1] We navigate pages according to their physical arrangement as well as according to their content, deciding what is proper to the text— we draw the boundary around the sovereign narrative, as well as the many lines of movement we can set out on in and out of that boundaried text.

Is it important to know about the rufous hornbill to understand its function in the *Noli*? Are the Two Gentleman, who appear in seven epigraphs in *Middlemarch*, a kind of chorus, and if so, why does the novel need this dramatic apparatus? Does Parr Traill make what is now Ontario more legible to her British readers through her annotations of berries and birds? One note instructs us to visit the British museum to see a taxidermied Canadian partridge: should such field trips be necessary to adequately read fiction? In each case, there is a question of where fictions begin and end, and how the production of knowledge may be inherently metaleptic: we need to imagine something *and* to find something, to decide *what* to read (what really counts as the text, since paratexts are often regarded as optional) and how far to go beyond the text one needs to go to adequately "read" it. A

1. Philip E. Steinberg, "Sovereignty, Territory, and the Mapping of Mobility: A View from Outside," *Annals of the Association of American Geographers* 99, no. 3 (July 2009): 474.

literal map of a fictional place—El Dorado—will conclude this chapter as an example of a kind of spatially realized metalepsis: an Austrian explorer uses an outmoded method of surveying to prove the existence of a place—El Dorado—that is already, by the beginning of the nineteenth century, regarded as mythical.

The Metafictional George Eliot

Wordsworth, the poet Wordsworth as Mr. Brooke clarifies it for us, appears in what are apparently two diegetic levels in *Middlemarch*. What is he doing in this novel? How can he be there? Nicholas Paige has recently asserted that "the mixture of historical precision and fabricated characters is intuitively novelistic."[2] We have historical characters in fictional places having dinner with fictional characters. We have fictional characters that fight in actual wars. We have places like Hardy's Wessex that float just above an actual Dorset and allow us to retrace Jude's steps into Christminster/Oxford with his tragic cakes via maps available from the thriving Hardy tourism industry. Retracing Jude's steps ought to cause us some consternation: there are no footsteps, after all, but instead it's a perfectly acceptable vacation plan. Catherine Gallagher has argued that it is the realistic novel's firm connection to the stuff of the real that makes us feel so secure about its ontology and our own: that is to say, we feel more real because the fictional cannot be realized or materialized: "Because George Eliot makes us imagine, not an independently living and breathing Dorothea, but instead an idea called Dorothea requiring that we conceive her bodily sensations to make her real, our very organic reality becomes newly discursive."[3] The implication might be that the novel seems less real as it convinces us of our own embodied-ness and that

2. Nicholas Paige, "The Impossible Princess: On (Not) Making Literary History," *PMLA* 125, no. 4 (October 2010): 1063.

3. Catherine Gallagher, "George Eliot, Immanent Victorian," *Representations* 90, no. 1 (Spring 2005): 73.

realism's wholly discursive quality soothes us at its own expense. Or, these two ontologies offer us a space in which to dwell—the bounded narrative, and a space in which we can crisscross from the story to the outside world and back again at will, enacting a kind of superhuman agency with the help of the kind of cartographic birds-eye view the novel offers.

As Brad Pasanek and Chad Wellmon argue in "The Enlightenment Index," "[C]ross-references are the sinews that connect and coordinate an ever-expanding system of print; but they also imply a greater network of reference that exceeds any particular instantiation or node within the system."[4] This potential for bibliographic linking may occur at any moment of a text, but paratextual features foreground the possibility that a brief quote from John Donne might take us back to his entire oeuvre, the poets with whom he was associated, Christian poetry broadly defined, as well as any literature written by a clergy person. We might turn to T. S. Eliot's criticism of Donne and the other metaphysicals, and we might read Eliot's poetry in connection with them. Similarly, a footnote about a bird might take us on an ornithological, environmental, imperial research excursion that could last for years. Paratexts make us appreciate a bibliographic sublime that lurks in every text, and which historicist criticism has only begun to restore to the realist novel.

The Diegetic Disruptions of the Poet Wordsworth

In *Middlemarch*, Wordsworth is both a character and an epigraph writer. At the beginning of chapter 2, Mr. Brooke tells us that "years ago" he dined with Wordsworth and Sir Humphry Davy, the inventor of the Davy lamp. "I was at Cambridge when Wordsworth was there, and I never met him—and I dined with

4. Brad Pasanek and Chad Wellmon, "The Enlightenment Index," *The Eighteenth Century* 56, no. 3 (Fall 2015): 363.

him twenty years afterwards at Cartwright's. There's an oddity in things."[5] But the plot thickens, if we take the paratext into the plot. Wordsworth also appears in the epigraphs, as an author of two of them. (He is also one of the originators of the self-authored epigraph—Scott is the other—of which Eliot was such a prolific producer. Of the eighty-six epigraphs in *Middlemarch*, Eliot writes thirty, Wordsworth writes two, and the rest are divided among Dante, Shakespeare, Pascal, Donne, Bunyan, and many others from Eliot's copious reading and commonplacing.)

It may be that a dinner with Wordsworth is a figment of Brooke's imagination (although, strictly speaking, Brooke does not have an imagination): Brooke is, after all, unreliable and likely to say anything at any moment. Does this make Wordsworth a fictional character? In the 1860s, there was no rider on the copyright page of the novel that proclaimed its fictionality; indeed, the nineteenth century is the resting place between claiming that the novel is factual and insisting that it's fictional.

John Plotz notes that characters in Eliot's novels often seem to be reading the chapter epigraphs such that one can imagine a stage version of the novel with the epigraphs hanging like so many cue cards around the periphery of the stage.[6] This would make the paratexts continuous with the text, in a kind of unfolded ontological origami. But what if Wordsworth is imagined reading the epigraphs attributed to him? Eliot has created a kind of divine metalepsis in which a character could encounter himself in another layer of the text: Wordsworth, at dinner with Mr. Brooke, looks up and sees part of his "Ode to Duty" hanging "above" the chapter. Or, is Eliot testing the idea of the "world" of the novel, directly connecting it to the world outside of it and insisting on breaches that remind us not only of textuality, but also of a vast system of intertextuality that allows

5. George Eliot, *Middlemarch* (New York: Penguin, 2003), 16.
6. John Plotz, *Semi-Detached: The Aesthetics of Virtual Experience since Dickens* (Princeton, NJ: Princeton University Press, 2018), 112–14.

us to read novels like *Middlemarch*? The Victorian novel is routinely described as encyclopedic, but if we go back to the literal encyclopedias that proliferated in the eighteenth century, we see that the practice of the epigraph suggests that Eliot was working on and from a vast network of textual traces. She seems keen to leave the maximum number and kind of traces herself, scattering as much text as she can.

Perhaps her method is rehearsed, or previewed, in the epigraph to *The Mill on the Floss*. The title page presents us with an epigraph: "In their death they were not divided." This "motto," as she often called her epigraphs, appears on the title page just under the author's pseudonym. The epigraph is distinctly paratextual, and yet it moves inside the diegesis by the novel's end and becomes an epitaph, set off with a dash and centered after a line break, and placed in quotation marks.[7] We end with the information that these words appear below the names of the siblings Tom and Maggie Tulliver on "the tomb."[8] This movement suggests that the first incidence of these words is not a paratext, but rather opens the novel to the world of the title page, which is the reader's world and theoretically separate: the world in which one reads versus the world about which one reads, to paraphrase Genette.[9] This system of citation usefully (for my argument) confounds our sense of a coherent diegesis.

Wordsworth may not have been too keen on participating in this tumbling literary ontology. He loomed large in Eliot's intellectual and emotional life: she read all of his poetry at an early age, purchased a six-volume set at the age of twenty-one, and only Shakespeare figures more often in her work.[10] Wordsworth

---

7. Laura Green pointed this out to me, personal communication.

8. George Eliot, *The Mill on the Floss* (1860; repr., Harmondsworth: Penguin, 1996), 522.

9. Gérard Genette, *Narrative Discourse: An Essay in Method*, trans. Jane E. Lewin (Ithaca, NY: Cornell University Press, 1980).

10. See Margaret Reynolds, introduction to *Adam Bede*, by George Eliot (Harmondsworth: Penguin, 2008).

is a moral touchstone in both *Adam Bede* and *Felix Holt*, in both of which a lack of understanding of *Lyrical Ballads* is seen as a symptom of ethical failing.[11] In *The Natural History of German Life*, Wordsworth is hailed, with Scott and Kingsley, as someone who draws the common people from life rather than from literature: he, like Eliot, is a student of provincial life. Paradoxically, Wordsworth was one of the most vocal Romantics when it comes to the kind of proliferation of print Eliot's novels perform: "quit your books, / or surely you'll grow double," he writes in "The Tables Turned," meaning doubled under their weight, but also perhaps enlarged in some insalubrious fashion.[12] As we saw in the introduction, for many critics, the Victorian novel was doubled (at least) beyond a reasonable size. Eliot may have loved Wordsworth's poetry, but it is uncertain as to whether Wordsworth would have loved Eliot's novels—he may have had to quit them and their avalanche of print. Nothing is left out, it seems, or, as Virginia Woolf puts it in a modernist moment of contempt regarding some mid-Victorian novelists, "Nothing would persuade them to concentrate. Able by nature to spin sentence after sentence melodiously, they seem to have left out nothing that they knew how to say."[13]

Wordsworth resides in three diegetic levels of *Middlemarch*: in Eliot's psyche (which Genette would consider a paratext itself), in the paratext, and in the diegesis. This is an ontological impossibility that the novel as a genre regularly enables. The omniscient narrator, for example, can regularly parachute into the diegesis for a bout of free indirect discourse or philosophical discussion in the first person. Once the map is drawn, the

11. Michal Peled Ginsburg, "Pseudonym, Epigraphs, and Narrative Voice: *Middlemarch* and the Problem of Authorship," *ELH* 47, no. 3 (Autumn 1980): 542–58.

12. William Wordsworth and Samuel Taylor Coleridge, *Lyrical Ballads*, ed. R. L. Brett and A. R. Jones (New York: Routledge, 2005), 149.

13. Virginia Woolf, review of *Mrs Gaskell: Haunts, Homes, and Stories*, by Ellis Chadwick. Woolf's review was first published in *The Times Literary Supplement*, September, 29, 1910.

boundaries are not inviolable. Indeed, they are particularly permeable, even in that apparently coherently diegetic fiction that we call realism, in which we imagine a (mostly) sealed off diegesis with an omniscient narrator in an extradiegetic layer and ourselves outside the whole contraption. Or at least this is a construction we have inherited from the criticism and history of the novel, making realism a more perfect form than it could have ever hoped to be given its early critical reception.

Is Eliot satirizing the presence of historical characters in fiction? That would seem to be too strong of a claim, except that a satirical character brings these others into the novel, and we don't know whether to believe him. I'll switch from Eliot to the novel to avoid this attribution of intention and say that the novel seems to be asking us to think about this ontological impossibility.

If Wordsworth is a historical character in the fictional world of the novel, what about the recurrence of the Two Gentleman, who appear in seven epigraphs, "speaking" like a kind of Greek chorus or a set of very short Spark notes? Are these two "characters"? Certainly they are fictional, or perhaps more rightly, they are abstract. Why do we need them? Johanna Drucker has argued that "basic graphic features organize the presentation of the textual elements, even though they are presumably extra-diegetic."[14] Eliot's epigraphs are centered above the beginning of each chapter, suggesting their separation from the narrative proper. They split the site and sight of reading, suggesting, as David Leon Higden has argued, that "one confronts the author in a persona in addition to the narration within the chapter"—a situation, he goes on to point out, that Henry James experienced as a " 'want of tact.' "[15] Are the epigraphs written by the author (well, yes, many of them are), and if so, then who is the narrator?

14. Joanna Drucker, "Graphic Devices: Narration and Navigation," *Narrative* 16, no. 2 (2008): 121–39, 121.

15. David Leon Higdon, "George Eliot and the Art of the Epigraph," *Nineteenth-Century Literature* 25, no. 2 (September 1970): 128.

That is, is the narrator another kind of writer, as it were, one who cannot be terse and prophetic? In their first appearance, at the head of chapter 4, the First Gentleman's line is "Our deeds are fetters that we forge ourselves." The Second Gentleman replies, "Ay, truly: but I think it is the world / That brings them."[16] Do these lines suggest the "meaning" of this chapter? Or comment on it, a general comment to enlarge our sympathy, as many of us think Eliot is wont to do? The epigraphs of *Middlemarch* add meaning, take up space, seem at times to substitute for the narrative, or make the narrative a kind of illustration of a pithy point Eliot did not expect us to get except by example. To return to Drucker: "Graphic devices encode models of reading, and the means of navigating a textual environment. They delimit the ground on which the figure of narrative emerges. They are the workings of the stage for the action. And then, they articulate the actions through the distinctions and relations they support."[17] In this dramatizing of the page, graphic and typological elements are a kind of material support for the "figure" of narrative. But can the ink and the narrative be this separable? The analysis of the materiality of texts has yielded great riches, but the separations that ensue—between book and text, for example—may sometimes be too great for the actual process of reading: we may miss "how imaginative works of literature have contributed to our understanding of books" as well as how "literature thinks in and about books."[18]

The epigraph seems optional, and yet in many cases it is a key or an aphorism that might belong in a commonplace book: a "beauty" or gem for the keepsake (and indeed many of Eliot's autographic epigraphs were thus collected). These Two Gentlemen are wiser than the Middlemarch gossips, perhaps: but they

16. Eliot, *Middlemarch*, 35.

17. Drucker, "Graphic Devices," 136.

18. Andrew Piper, *Dreaming in Books: The Making of the Bibliographic Imagination in the Romantic Age* (Chicago: University of Chicago Press, 2009), 10 and 11.

also create a diegetic problem on the page. Are they in or out of the story? They are certainly in the novel, and Eliot writes them. Why does she seem to need at least two ways to "tell" each chapter? As Genette points out,

> [W]e must not forget that the very notion of paratext . . . has more to do with a decision about method than with a truly established fact. "The paratext," properly speaking, does not *exist*; rather, one chooses to *account in these terms* for a certain number of practices or effects. . . . The question is therefore not whether the note does or does not "belong" to the paratext but really whether considering it in such a light is or is not useful and relevant.[19]

Eliot's paratexts seem to belong outside the diegesis, but they remind us, as Eirian Yem has argued, that the epigraphs subvert realism by drawing attention to the break between text and paratext: "The novel, like the archive, captures that which is enunciated in the gaps between all the information collected."[20] The gaps are the index that can never be tabulated, but which we need to have somewhere in mind. The blank space between epigraph and narrative reminds us not only that there may be something missing from the narrative, but also how much novels like *Middlemarch* are themselves archives and anthologies, acquisitive and aspirational by turns.

The Bird Footnote

In many annotated editions of novels, footnotes are essentially definitions, but these definitions don't do much for us until we attach a web of connotations to them.[21] When you see a footnote

19. Genette, *Paratexts*, 343.
20. Eirian Yem, "'A Peculiar Tongue of Their Own': Epigraphs in George Eliot's Late Novels" (master's thesis, Oxford University, 2017), 34.
21. See Elaine Freedgood and Cannon Schmitt, "Introduction: Technically, Denotatively, Literally," *Representations* 125, no. 1 (2014): 1–14.

for an archaic object, or an arcane historical location, or a translation of a non-English word, we feel "informed," and historically and linguistically enlightened. Bird footnotes seemed to me, initially, like a dead end because they are about "nature," the historicity of which is easy to forget. They seem simply like strangely opaque visual aids that cannot possibly have any impact on our understanding of a novel.

In Parr Traill's *Canadian Crusoes* (1852), three teenagers (two British and one French) get lost in the woods of Ontario and cheerfully recapitulate the development of civilization with much-needed help from a Mohawk girl, and then find their way home.[22] Parr Trail footnotes a moment when Louis, the French teen, finds some partridge eggs: "the Canadian partridge is a species of grouse, larger than the English or French partridge. We refer our young readers to the finely arranged specimens in the British museum (open to the public) where they may discover 'Louis's partridge.'"[23] The idea seems to be that one can put down the novel, go to the museum, and then come back to the novel with the bird in mind. More immediately, the footnote guarantees very literally that the novel is firmly connected, as Catherine Gallagher has put it, to the stuff of the real, in this case with an extratextual grouse in London.[24]

But why does Parr Traill make the comparison between the Canadian Partridge and the English Partridge? A grouse is not a partridge, for one thing, so Parr Traill and her fellow settlers have essentially, Adam-like, renamed a species and helped a newly forming nation invent "indigenous creatures." But even the English partridge can hardly be granted a national identity: surely they may occasionally step into Wales or Scotland, or hop

22. For a reading of this novel, see Elaine Freedgood, "Fictions of Settlement: Footnotes, Metalepsis and the Colonial Effect," *NLH* 41, no. 2 (Spring 2010): 393–411.

23. Catherine Parr Strickland Traill, *Lost in the Backwoods: A Tale of the Canadian Forest* (New York: T. Nelson and Sons, 1882), 40.

24. Gallagher, "George Eliot: Immanent Victorian," 74.

a ship for Calais or the Caribbean. More confusingly still, the English partridge is also known as the Hungarian partridge. I think the idea of Canadian birds helps to naturalize the idea of "Canada" and grants an odd kind of sovereignty to creatures that has been stripped from indigenous people, like the Mohawk girl whom the teens name, with great flair, Indiana.

The Philippine hornbill (or rufous hornbill) is endemic to two islands of that archipelago; thus it is in a sense Philippine, but only after the fact, I would guess, since again, statehood certainly came after the hornbill. *Noli Me Tangere*, or the *Noli* as it is called in the Philippines, is the novel that is seen as the beginning of the decolonization of the Philippines and is the opening example of a national community imagining itself in Benedict Anderson's *Imagined Communities*. Anderson quotes the opening three paragraphs of the novel in which a dinner party and the house in which it will be given are discussed; he then goes on to note that

> right from the start of the image (wholly new to Filipino writing) of a dinner party being discussed by hundreds of unnamed people, who do not know each other, in quite different parts of Manila, in a particular month of a particular decade, immediately conjures up the imagined community. And in the phrase "a house on 'Anloague Street'" which 'we shall describe in such a way that it may still be recognized,'" the would-be recognizers are we-Filipino-readers.[25]

Like the grouse in the British museum, we have a field trip at hand, a place to visit that vouches for the realness of two communities: the characters in the novel and the people reading it who know Manila and Anloague Street.

Rizal wrote in Spanish and left certain words in Tagalog, but used none of the many other local languages, thereby reducing

25. Benedict Anderson, *Imagined Communities: Reflections on the Origin and Spread of Nationalism*, rev. ed. (London: Verso, 2006), 27.

the non-Filipino's sense of the linguistic diversity of the islands radically, although making it seem, for a reader like me, culturally and linguistically exotic. Sometimes Rizal translates a Tagalog word in the text. An early translator of the novel into English would translate the Tagalog into English phrases, in the text, without the Tagalog word. In the edition I have, the editor, Harold Augenbraum, has translated many Tagalog words in footnotes, as well as many Latin phrases, historical personages, places, and so on.[26] There is a randomness to footnotes, a contingency of the moment of annotation and the idea of what "needs" to be noted. That contingency might also be called history. And the languages that need "translation" are multiple— many of them without official names.

The hornbill in the note is a translation of the Tagalog "Kalauy." It was not Philippine at the time of the novel because only Filipinos who lived in Spain (*illustrados*) called themselves by this national designation. People in the Philippines were more likely to call themselves by their tribal or pueblo group. So the translation is anachronistic, and suggests a sense of "local color" that does not yet exist.

The Philippine hornbill is threatened with extinction now (because of deforestation), but when the hornbill was more plentiful, it was a kind of time keeper, calling out the beginning and end of the work day, breakfast and dinner, the coming of darkness, and in one chapter, the danger of darkness for two children who are not yet home. In the *Noli*, the hornbill is a kind of Philippine barometer—literally in that it serves a mechanical function—and a counterpart of the barometer in Flaubert's *A Simple Heart*, which Roland Barthes uses to argue that some things in fiction simply indicate the real and have no other meaning.[27]

26. José Rizal, *Noli Me Tangere (Touch Me Not)*, ed. Harold Augenbraum (New York: Penguin, 2006).

27. Roland Barthes, "The Reality Effect," in *The Rustle of Language*, trans. Richard Howard (Berkeley: University of California Press, 1984).

Much more avian attention is paid in the *Noli* to the lucrative cock fights that take up an entire, highly acerbic chapter (the cockfighting ring is nicer than the school), and which are mentioned frequently throughout the novel. They need no footnote, because cockfights are nearly universal, I guess, but one could be written about the fact that although the Spanish did not introduce cock fighting to the Philippines, they regulated and taxed it and made huge profits from it.[28]

A third example comes from Kipling's *Kim*. Few of the major characters in *Kim* are indigenous to South Asia, or even native. Kim is Irish; the lama is Tibetan. But Kim, in a typical imperial fantasy, "passes" for native when he wishes to and has the kind of entrée to all levels of the social world of colonial India that make him an agile participant in the Great Game. At one point, in Edward Said's edition for Penguin, a mynah bird is footnoted, again in a translation, as "the Indian starling."[29] This is in a conversation between the lama, Kim, and a sort of client of the lama who wants a cure for her sick son. Kim tries to defend the lama against performing such an act, which is unholy. The woman compares Kim (unfavorably) to a mynah, which can imitate anyone (suggesting that Kim's "passing" may not be as successful as he thinks). Indeed, the mynah, like the starling, the parrot, and indeed many sparrows, is an excellent mimic. Like Kim, it is also extremely rugged, adaptable, and will walk bravely through traffic.

The word and the bird are originally South Asian (the word is Hindi), but the mynah has now migrated and adapted extremely well to much of the Anglophone world and thus, like so many other Hindi words, "mynah" is now also an English word. The crested mynah arrived in Vancouver, according to the Audubon

28. Scott Guggenheim, "Cock or Bull: Cockfighting, Social Structure and Political Commentary in the Philippines," *Filipinas* 3, no. 1 (1982): 1–33.

29. Rudyard Kiping, *Kim*, ed. Edward W. Said (New York: Penguin, 1989), 361n17.

website,[30] in 1897—the website does not tell us how this precise date is known—a ship's manifest, perhaps? Mynas were introduced to Australia to control locusts, but are now called "invasive colonizers."[31] It is legal to kill them because they are "registered pests," and in Googling "mynah" and "empire," I found a jeweler, Emily Valentine, who makes jewelry out of feathers, but can't keep up a sufficient supply with road kill and dead pets alone, so began trapping mynahs:

> I have been trapping the registered pest, the indian mynah bird and using the feathers. With these, I made *Mynah Collie* 2007, a feathered dog, one of my dog flu series, and it was awarded a merit prize in the **Norseweart**, the New Zealand Contemporary Art Award. I have been using the mynah birds for my new ***Squadron Series*** (groups of small planes for the wall). This series compares the military invasion with the invasion of non-indigenous species.[32]

There is a special charm in Valentine, as the descendant of white settlers, comparing military invasion with the "invasion of non-indigenous species." The Indian mynah (Valentine doesn't capitalize "Indian" for some reason) was deliberately introduced into Australia (and many other British colonies). They did not decide to invade the place themselves.

Reading bird footnotes is not a form of interpretation. These footnotes, when we read them, and especially when we read them as a genre, form a shadow, a penumbra of often devastating information that attends the novel. They suggest further

30. "Crested Myna," National Audubon Society, https://www.audubon.org/field-guide/bird/crested-myna.

31. Jennifer Nichols and Scott Lamond, "Call to Trap 'Exploding' Populations of Indian Myna Birds," *ABC Rural*, September 8, 2016, https://www.abc.net.au/news/rural/2016-09-08/indian-myna-birds-pest-species/7819394.

32. "Home," Emily Valentine, updated 2012, https://emilyvalentine.com.au/index.html.

footnoting; they suggest that definitions contain histories, as dictionary entries so often demonstrate. I'm suggesting that we read footnotes (and not only those about birds) separately, as a genre, which of course they are—"A Footnote" or "Notes" are frequent scholarly and literary genres, although not quite in the way I am suggesting here. The information about birds is not what the novel is "about." And yet, the note offers us a form of writing that does not commit itself to closure or argument—although it may end up offering us both—but in which powerful forms of knowledge have been transmitted, from the footnotes in early modern alchemical journals to James Baldwin's *Notes of a Native Son*. The tentative, modest, and optional nature of the footnote can be a space to fray the edges of novels, orthodoxies, and histories.

The novel offers us at least three histories: the time of its writing, the time in which it takes place, and the time in which we read it. We might add the moment of annotation as a fourth time. If we follow the birds, the fish, the goats, the fruit, and the trees out of the novel and into journals of forestry, biology, ecology, and so on, we find a history of ecological imperialism in the form of the transport of pets, the introduction of species for biological pest control, and the random movements of species on ships and shoes, which is now often being told, by "invasion biologists," as a history of a kind of allegorical illegal immigration.[33] It also creates a narrative of indignation about indigeneity that does not extend to indigenous people.

Nineteenth-century novels contain this history (although they don't recount it), because at a certain point early in that century, Harriet Ritvo has argued, nature became less fearful to

33. For the typical "invasion" narrative, see Michael Marchetti and Peter B. Moyle, *Protecting Life on Earth: An Introduction to the Science of Conservation* (Berkeley: University of California Press, 2010). For a sharp critique of metaphors of invasion, see Brendan Larson, *Metaphors for Environmental Sustainability: Redefining Our Relationship with Nature* (New Haven, CT: Yale University Press, 2011).

humans, and birds and fish and trees became attached to a nostalgic idea of place and attained national identities.[34] The action of *Kim*, for example, may take place at a time before mynahs have become international settlers, but at the time of writing, Kipling may well have known how successful the mynah had become as an introduced or invasive bird in the settler colonies and so how much resonance and comedy the comparison of this mimicking, peripatetic, rugged bird would have had to Kim himself. At the time of annotation, in 1984, of my Penguin edition, the issue is one of translation. I can now write a note on the footnote, complete with the murderous feather jeweler of the myna, because of current technologies of searching text, and because of the many turns in materialist, ecological, and postcolonial criticism that have influenced me. The history of the representation of the living matter of the novel can extend before and after the times of the novel, suggesting that local color and the particularities of place may be no such thing, and that before the ship and the plane, the storm and raft of floating timber made sure that even regional, much less national identities were imagined, and sometimes best imagined in the life of novels. The novel, especially in its nineteenth-century form, promises us places we cannot see, not only because they are gone, but because they never existed except in the cartographical fine-tuning that only fictional representation can provide. Turning denotation into connotation, following birds out of footnotes, creating our own footnotes for birds not noted, creates an unwitting historical novel with an ongoing plot.

Refusing the Territory of the Novel

We have the wild metalepses of the eighteenth century and of postmodern fiction, which are brazen and comic and which

34. Harriet Ritvo, *The Animal Estate: The English and Other Creatures in the Victorian Age* (Cambridge, MA: Harvard University Press, 1987), 3.

underscore fictionality and the difficulty of reference. And then in the nineteenth century, what Franco Moretti calls in *The Bourgeois* the "serious century," an even more radical metalepsis develops and is simultaneously tamed into invisibility.[35] We learn, because each reader's ontogeny of reading recapitulates the phylogeny of literary criticism, to just jump over, like so many small puddles, the existential crevasses, the ontological breaches of realism, and to experience all the facts in the novel as references (if we are naïve, or naïvely realist), on the one hand, or (on another hand that is so different it might as well be a foot) reality effects of one kind or another. We can toggle back and forth between reference and reality effect: it is a problem that cannot be solved because it is endemic to the novel, especially the ones that we call realistic.

Novelistic mimesis with this kind of crazed diegetic layering is important to have on hand because, for so many projects of knowledge *and* of disinformation, the seamless mix of the observed and the imagined are essential. In D. Graham Burnett's *Masters of All They Surveyed: Exploration, Geography and a British El Dorado*,[36] we learn how a mediocre but incredibly dogged nineteenth-century Viennese explorer called Robert Schomburgk set out to "verify" Raleigh's discovery of El Dorado (even though it was understood to be a myth by the early nineteenth century), and then provided a "map" of it (a paratext) for a new edition of Raleigh's text, which was entitled the *Discovery of the Large, Rich and Beautiful Empire of Guiana*. Fiction joins fact and El Dorado is "found." This is then used by the British to claim sovereignty over certain highly contested borders between British Guiana and Venezuela. Schomburgk attempts to make British Guiana the ground zero, the very first colony, of the British Empire, although Raleigh was never actually in

35. Franco Moretti, *The Bourgeois: Between History and Literature* (New York: Verso, 2013), 13.

36. D. Graham Burnett, *Masters of All They Surveyed: Exploration, Geography and a British El Dorado* (Chicago: University of Chicago Press, 2000).

what became British Guiana, and the *Discovery* is a poem with fictional contents.

Schomburgk used the traverse method of surveying, the one most widely used in the eighteenth century when the chains of the English civil surveyor (like those of Caleb Garth) could not be hauled through swamps, jungles, and over mountains. The traverse method is particularly metaleptic: "As coordinates in the graticule of longitude and latitude, every fixed point had been postulated by the blank map before it was observed on the ground. . . . To have geographical significance, every fixed point had to be linked to a point on the ground." In short, an abstract set of graticules is articulated with points on the ground that are being viewed not by the eyes of birds, but by the eyes of men walking on the ground. How actual points on very difficult ground will find their "real" match with a graticule on a diagram is a problem, and, as we might expect, Schomburgk's maps were not very reliable.[37]

Mapping and surveying are crucial activities of what is called the modern period. James Scott writes, "[T]he premodern state was in many crucial respects blind; it knew precious little about its subjects, their wealth, their landholdings and yields, their location, their very identity. It lacked anything like a detailed 'map' of its terrain and its people."[38] (I'm not sure the modern or postmodern state has solved this problem either.) It is easy to imagine the novel, especially the novels considered in this chapter, as part of this process of mapping at the level of content (in fact, there is mapping at the level of content in *Middlemarch*: as I have just noted, Caleb Garth is a surveyor). But it is at the level

37. The triangular survey, the more reliable method of the nineteenth century and the one used to map India, required too much cumbersome equipment for this undercapitalized adventurer.

38. James Scott, *Seeing Like a State: How Certain Schemes to Improve the Human Condition Have Failed* (New Haven, CT: Yale University Press, 1998), 184; qtd. in Stuart Elden, *The Birth of Territory*, (Chicago: University of Chicago Press, 2013), 325.

of form that things perhaps get the most interesting: "space only becomes territory through acts of bounding and making visible," James Corner writes.[39] In representation, when diegetic boundaries are traversed, that is not a literally *cartographic* act, but it is one that contributes to the cartographic imagination: "For territory to be meaningful it has to be reproduced by the enactment of challenges to it, by questionings and erasures of boundaries as markers of space, but also through the inscription of new boundaries."[40] But the important thing for our purposes is that the process of creating territory, of making worlds, is metaleptic: it depends on rupture and proliferation through imagined connections of points on a grid and points on the ground.[41] Thongchai Winichakul points out in *Siam Mapped* that

> In terms of most communication theories and common sense, a map is a scientific abstraction of reality. A map merely represents something which already exists and is objectively "there." In the history I have described this relationship was reversed. A map anticipated spatial reality, not vice versa. In other words, a map was a model for, rather than a model of, what it purported to represent.[42]

We might say in turn that diegesis anticipates existential reality, but only through ruptures that make existential spaces available as discrete units. But these borders, a recent invention as are other kinds of borders, are drawn and not found.

Adela Pinch adumbrates the problem of triangulation in fiction as similar to those of the geographer and cartographer:

> Triangulation may be described, then, as a process of using a very limited fund of information . . . about reality in order to

39. James Corner, "The Agency of Mapping: Speculation, Critique and Invention," in *Mappings*, ed. Dennis Cosgrove (London: Reaktion, 1999), 222; qtd. in Elden, *Birth of Territory*, 327.

40. Steinberg, "Sovereignty, Territory, and the Mapping of Mobility."

41. Burnett, *Masters of All They Surveyed*, 15.

42. Qtd. in Anderson, *Imagined Communities*, 173.

extrapolate a more complete picture. Described this way, "triangulation" might also describe as well the process by which, according to the theories of literary realism . . . readers take the partial limited cues of realist fiction and from thence extrapolate a world.[43]

Pinch goes on to quote a mid-Victorian engineering guide that recommends "imagining" as good practice for getting from the "theoretical" to the "practical."[44] So that reading the world and reading the novel are on a "continuum" rather than taking place in two different ontological planes.[45]

Pinch's ideas about triangulation land us all in the same place: imagining the world is a way of living in it. Our reading of metalepsis in fiction might help us to understand borders as elaborate conceits, as lines that are drawn and redrawn and cannot reliably guide us forward. Wordsworth can exist in every diegetic level of *Middlemarch* because there are, ultimately, no such "levels," except in narrative theory. Omniscient narrators can intrude because they are not outside the diegesis or blocked by its existential constraints. The novel, which takes us beyond fact and deception, also takes us beyond the boundaries of a modernity that is a fantasy for the ideological and physical mapping of empire. If the territory becomes the map, the novel is the diagram of the end of territory if we read it outside of period and place, if we discard realism and all of our claims about *the* Victorian novel. Novels emerge as disruptors of our conventional ideas about knowledge and ways of knowing, although they suggest that the production of knowledge is often, if not always, metaleptic: that we have a graticule in mind and try to find its correspondent on the ground. The novel understands our reliance on the relationship between the two in the making of what

43. Adela Pinch, "Reality-Sensing in Elizabeth Gaskell, or Half-Mended Stockings," *ELH* 83, no. 3 (Fall 2016): 826.

44. Ibid.

45. Ibid.

we call, often with too much confidence, knowledge. One strategy for intervening in this process is to keep bibliographic metalepsis alive: to read beyond, and further, and in what may be critically unacceptable ways. Beyond surface and depth, there is a vast library, and even though most of its texts are missing, we can make use of what is there and what is implicitly indicated as archived in the many gaps between texts.

Hetero-Ontologicality

Preamble

"No competent reader picking up *Crime and Punishment* has any trouble recognizing the murder as invented and the locale, Saint Petersburg, as real," Peter J. Rabinowitz writes.[1] The realist novel is ruptured by its twin commitments to fictionality and reference: fictional murders in actual geographical locations, plots interrupted by historical wars, historical characters walking into fictional dinner parties. It is this kind of rupture, and the "worlds" that such ruptures proliferate, that gives the multilayered, embodied, and ensouled liberal subject practice in the imaginary conquest of space and time. I am going to argue in what follows that the novel—an imperial genre at the highest level of formal abstraction, and at the most basic level of content—teaches us the practices of space and time that allow us to imagine and enact expansion and colonization—of territory, of the future, of other minds.

This ontological flexibility is also a discursive one: it allows us to decide what is historically accurate and what is purely or only fictional on a case-by-case basis. Is Jane Eyre a typical

---

1. Peter J. Rabinowitz, "Assertion and Assumption: Fictional Patterns and the External World," *PMLA* 96, no. 3 (1981): 412.

governess? Does Madame Bovary have to die? Can *The Posthumous Memoirs of Bras Cubas* make a claim to realistic representation given the existential impossibility of its narration? Does it record something about Brazilian slavery that a more conventionally realist text could not? When Roberto Bolaño offers police report-like of deaths in what he admits in interviews to be Ciudad Juarez, but which in *2066* he calls Santa Theresa, are these deaths historical material within the novel?[2] Or is the novel—as a genre, as a realist form—the source of the kind of reports it re-presents? We have a seemingly infinite flexibility in deciding these questions, bringing literary and social, historical and generic, linguistic and political material to bear on our interpretations. This practice—of deciding on the truth in fiction—reverberates in every instance of questioning and interpreting the forms of realism that have been decoupled from fictionality: news reports, journalistic photography, and official documents of all kinds, for example. We have a look at the "evidence," we develop opinions, and we give what seems like our very own considered consent to the institutions and ideologies of our world.

The realist fiction of the nineteenth century has been treated by critics, and I think experienced by readers, as an oasis from the zany ruptures of fiction that is not yet or nor longer realistic precisely because of its referentiality. If we did notice the madcap metaleptic adventures between history and fiction, it would create, I think, a vertiginous hetero-ontologicality, which I will discuss in the following section. Every sentence in which a fictional character traverses an actual city or an actual poet has dinner with a fictional character or an actual war is observed or fought in by a fictional character is a rupture of enormous existential proportions. That such ruptures do not feel like ruptures may be the most significant thing about them.

<hr/>

2. Roberto Bolano, *The Last Interview*, trans. Sybil Pecz. (Brooklyn: Melville House, 2006), 96, discussing Roberto Bolaño, *2666: A Novel*, trans. Natasha Wimmer (New York: Picador, 2009).

Hetero-Ontologicality

So two characters walk into a bar. One is fictional, the other historical. So far, so good, according to most literary theory of the past hundred or so years. The fictional character can do whatever she wants to do. The historical character, in order to retain her already-lived story, has to remain in a pretty shadowy background, and above all, she cannot speak. Alessandro Manzoni contends, in his 1927 study, *On the Historical Novel*, that tragedy cannot be historical because in tragedy "it is only poetry that speaks";[3] the discourses that Shakespeare, Corneille, and Voltaire put into the mouth of Caesar, for example, are— must be—poetic fabrications.[4] Lukács, in *The Historical Novel*, explains that in Scott's novels, historical greatness necessarily goes hand in hand with a minor compositional role.[5] In *S/Z*, Barthes argues that

> it is precisely [their] lesser importance which confers upon the historical personage his exact weight of reality ... for if the historical personage were to assume his real importance, the discourse would be obliged to endow him with a contingency which paradoxically, would make him less real ... it would only be necessary to make them speak, and like impostors, they would expose themselves.... Yet if they are merely mixed in with their fictional neighbors, mentioned as having simply been present at some social gathering, their modesty, like a lock between two levels of water, equalizes novel and history.... They are superlative effects of the real.[6]

3. Alessandro Manzoni, *On The Historical Novel*, trans. Sandra Bermann (1927; repr., Lincoln: University of Nebraska Press, 1984), 114–15.

4. Ibid., 115.

5. Georg Lukács, *The Historical Novel*, trans. Hannah Mitchell and Stanley Mitchell (Lincoln: University of Nebraska Press, 1962), 39.

6. Roland Barthes, *S/Z: An Essay*, trans. Richard Miller (New York: Farrar, Strauss, and Giroux, 1974), 102.

Reality effects, especially superlative ones, wobble on a knife-edge between fictionality and reference: the balance must be maintained as a lock maintains the balance between two levels of water, or the historical person becomes contingent.

In Thackeray's *The History of Henry Esmond*, Henry, thinking that the historical Lord Mohun is dead after falling from his horse, bleeds him and thereby revives him. Stephen Bann writes,

> Mohun not only happens not to be dead . . . but is necessarily not dead since his historical role is still to be played [that is, dying in a historically bloody duel that causes dueling laws to be changed, requiring that guns be used rather than swords]. Furthermore, the fact that Henry revives Mohun by bleeding him underlines the absurdity of the supposition that blood which is let by the penknife (the blood of fiction) can either diminish or strengthen the life which Mohun holds by a non-fictional guarantee.[7]

Lord Mohun and Henry can coexist comfortably in the same novel, but they cannot come this close together without making critics and many readers what George Eliot described as "uncomfortable."[8] (Charlotte Brontë called the novel "admirable and odious.")[9] There are several ways to be uncomfortable here: one can be uncomfortable with the novel, *Henry Esmond* locally, or with the historical novel generally, or with the novel as a genre altogether. And this discomfort might gather around the revelation of the figure that I think governs the historical and the realist novel with equal force: metalepsis.

Metalepsis, as discussed in the introduction, is a rupture of one ontological or diegetic layer into another. Realist and

7. Stephen Bann, *The Clothing of Clio: A Study of the Representation of History in Nineteenth-Century Britain and France* (Cambridge: Cambridge University Press, 1984), 149–50.

8. Eliot: To Mr. and Mrs. Charles Bray (November 13, 1852), George Eliot, *Letters*, ed. Gordon S. Haight (New Haven, CT: Yale University Press, 1954).

9. William Makepeace Thackeray, *The History of Henry Esmond, Esq.* (New York: Harper & Brothers, 1898), xxiii.

historical fiction are almost never accused of metalepsis, and certainly not on the grounds of reference, historical or otherwise. Referentiality has not been regarded as this kind of rupture. I want to argue that it *is* metalepsis, and that we make use of it unconsciously: we use it to establish multiple worlds in which to imagine the fictional and the referential; it gives us a kind of imminent and eminent domain over a reality that we get to construct according to our individualized, or apparently individualized, needs. Part of being a liberal subject, as Elaine Hadley has so brilliantly argued in *Living Liberalism*, is to develop a variety of opinions to entertain in the private theater of one's mind: opinions about what is fact and what is fiction are basic to this process.[10] The novel is a key technology in this, and it works because it produces an impossible ontology. The liberal subject, the idea of the liberal subject I should say, is itself an impossible ontology: see, for example, Simon Gikandi's *Slavery and the Culture of Taste* for a magisterial argument about the splitting of the emerging concepts of liberty, taste, and cultivation from concurrent practices of slavery, servitude, and violence in the eighteenth and nineteenth centuries.[11] The liberal subject needs worlds—a world of aesthetic autonomy, for example, and a world of plantation slavery—in which to dwell: that is already science fiction, we might say. Realism, nicely enough, provides worlds, and does so in a way we have come to experience as seamless, as realistic.

In certain apparently foolish or failed historical novels, the achieved contingency of historical persons is precisely the benefit of what otherwise seems to be a gaff. That is to say, the virtue of having the option to render historical characters contingent—of giving them fictional blood to spill, or alternate deaths to die, of allowing their histories to be rewritten—is that it offers a

10. See Elaine Hadley, *Living Liberalism: Practical Citizenship in Mid-Victorian Britain* (Chicago: University of Chicago Press, 2010), esp. chap. 3, "A Frame of Mind: Signature Liberalism in the *Fortnightly Review*."

11. Simon Gikandi, *Slavery and the Culture of Taste* (Princeton, NJ: Princeton University Press, 2011).

collective "what if" to the collective thinking about history. It opens a passage to counterfactuality, an exercise that reminds us that historical events might have unfolded otherwise.

Symptomatic Writing

One kind of novel that is uneasily and intensely fraught with counterfactuality comes from a subspecies of the historical novel that is particularly disturbing and disturbed: the Indian Mutiny Novel (also known as the Indian Rebellion Novel and the Novels of the First War of Independence).[12] This genre developed in response to the Indian rebellion of 1857, and which between the 1860s and the early twentieth century flourished and produced often hallucinatory rewritings and derealizations of a war that seemed impossible for the British to assimilate to their idea of their national and imperial history. Christopher Herbert, in his book on the Mutiny Novel, *War of No Pity*, drew my attention to the rupturedness of the genre in his description of the way that the "factual and the fantastic spiral dizzyingly together" in these works; note at the same time, however, that the following description is, in a sense, unremarkable and might be found in just about any "realistic" novel:

> Sometimes in these novels historical personages walk fantastically in under their own names from the supposed world of historical reality to play roles in the fictional dramas of make-believe protagonists; sometimes these historical personages mask themselves . . . in fictional incognitos that the

12. The Indian Mutiny Novel has been described as a genre by several critics: see, for example, Chakravarty and Herbert (Christopher Herbert, *War of No Pity: The Indian Mutiny and Victorian Trauma* [Princeton, NJ: Princeton University Press, 2009]; and Gautam Chakravarty, *The Indian Mutiny and the British Imagination* [Cambridge: Cambridge University Press, 2005]). The concept of genre is obviously fraught, but in different ways the above two critics have made a compelling case for a particularly pathological historicization that occurs in these novels that might earn them the category of genre.

reader is weirdly enough meant to immediately penetrate; sometimes historical documents, whether identified as such or not, are introduced verbatim into the made-up stories; and in all these stories, imaginary people move in the milieu of historical reality and live through real-life events.[13]

What Herbert describes in the Mutiny Novel might be ascribed uncontroversially to the historical novel since Edgeworth and Scott, and to the novel in general since its inception. The point is, I think, that not only do historical characters walk in and move in the milieu of historical reality; they, like Lord Mohun, become contingent. For one thing, they often speak.

One job of the Mutiny Novel seems to be to justify British violence in that war by imagining Indian violence as "without parallel in history," as G. A. Henty's narrator rather remarkably puts it in one of his two Mutiny Novels, *In Times of Peril*.[14] This violence consisted of the "slaughtering" and "massacring" of British women and children, always in "cold blood," and of the mass rape of British women by Indian men.[15] This last was imagined in all kinds of lurid fantasies, and many critics have commented on the pornographic quality of their detail and inventiveness. This tendency was most pronounced in the last years of the nineteenth century, the years of "high imperialism." The Mutiny Novel in these years in particular—which saw the advent of the boy's adventure novel—acted as a guarantor of British heroism in a war in which Indians were unscrupulous, duplicitous, and cowardly while British participants upheld the standards of a fair fight.

In what follows, I focus on Henty's other Mutiny Novel, *Rujub, the Juggler* (1893), which is much more complex than the generalizations above would suggest. Rujub, who is not the

13. Herbert, *War of No Pity*, 278–79.
14. G. A Henty, *In Times of Peril: A Tale of India* (London: Griffith and Farran, 1881), 22.
15. Ibid., 135.

protagonist of the novel but is still one of its heroes, is a mystic, a mesmerist, and a telepathist who saves the British romantic heroine of the novel, Isobel Hannay, from both the zenana or harem of the historical Nana Sahib, and the historical murder of women and children at his hands in a makeshift prison in Kanpur, or, as the British spelled it, Cawnpore.

The novel opens with a charming fete at the majestic home of Nana Sahib: "It would be difficult to find a fairer scene," the first sentence tells us.[16] Innumerable lights and lanterns are strung along paths, around a pond, among terraces, and all around the doors and windows of the "the Palace or Castle."[17] And yet in so much light, there is a heart of great darkness, although the British guests have no idea: "in all India there was no Rajah with more pronounced English tastes or greater affection for English people. . . . All this, as everyone said, was the more remarkable and praiseworthy, inasmuch as he had grounds of complaint against the British government."[18] The grounds of his complaint would be the annexation of his land by Lord Dalhousie, part of Dalhousie's land grabs in Oude in the mid-fifties, which contributed substantially to fomenting Nana Sahib's vigorous participation in the Indian rebellion. When the party is over, the Rajah reveals himself, in discussion with the commander of his troops and the head of his household: "little do they think what their good friend Nana Sahib is preparing for them. What a poor-spirited creature they think me to kiss the hand that robbed me of my rights. But the day of reckoning is not far off, and then woe to them all!"[19] Nana Sahib's duplicitousness is revealed in his own words. He goes on to describe the specific ways in which he has been generating rebellion—distributing mysterious (and threatening because mysterious) chapattis and spreading the rumor that cartridges in army-issued rifles had been greased

16. G. A. Henty, *Rujub, the Juggler* (New York: Hurst & Company, 1901), 1.
17. Ibid.
18. Ibid., 2.
19. Ibid., 3.

with pig fat. The greased cartridge, typically cited then as now as the proximate cause of the rebellion, is, as Gautam Chakravarty points out, "a metonymy for the culture of a pre-modern society locked in an 'invincible immobility.' "[20]

The novel soon leaves Rujub at his over-the-top castle, and picks up its many British characters—mostly part of a British regiment in the fictional Deennugghur—and soon a love interest evolves between Ralph Bathurst and a new and "fresh" arrival (such arrivals are always fresh) from England, Isobel Hannay, the niece of an army major bachelor, who has asked her to come out and keep house for him. Bathurst is a civil servant rather than an army officer because he is a "coward," "born with a constitutional horror of firearms" and other things that cause very loud noises.[21] Fortunately, the novel gives him a terrific opportunity to prove that his cowardice is limited and therefore not characterological when he saves Rabda, the daughter of Rujub the Juggler from a tiger, using a whip. (The tiger is too startled to roar.) This makes father and daughter alike thoroughly indebted to Bathurst, which is an amazingly lucky thing, as we'll see.

Rujub's psychic powers are displayed early on: in the beginning of the novel, he throws special powder on a fire and produces various seemingly inexplicable visions of the future, such as one in which Bathurst and Isobel are disguised as "natives," dyed brown and wearing native garb—visions that come true later in the novel.[22] He can perform various tricks of jugglers made famous in the British press of the nineteenth century, like the mango trick in which a three-foot-tall tree grows in moments from a seed, and, most helpfully, he can communicate with Bathurst telepathically, and Rabda can likewise communicate with Isobel, essentially changing the course of "history" within this fiction—the novel is based on a somewhat true story

---

20. Chakravarty, *The Indian Mutiny and the British Imagination*, 30.
21. Henty, *Rujub, the Juggler*, 179.
22. Ibid., 129.

of an actual army Major and his niece in the Mutiny. The niece was captured by the Nana Sahib and becomes part of his zenana, and apparently ended up married to one of her Muslim captors.

Rujub has been a supporter of the rebellion, although he modifies his view as the novel progresses, coming to realize that the British must administer India or the country will "be red with blood."[23] Still, a few chapters later, Rujub says to Bathurst of the Sepoys, "they are fighting for their freedom."[24] Bathurst blusters back, "They are fighting for nothing of the sort," and goes on a diatribe about Indians exchanging one set of masters for another.[25] But Rujub's statement, and his subject position, remains on the page, their elegant simplicity hardly gainsaid by Bathurst's rant. This kind of character is actually common in mutiny fiction, and perhaps "proves" how sympathetic certain English subjects can be—Bathurst, in his role as civil servant, is hard working and confesses to Isobel that "[w]hen you get to know the natives well you can't help liking them and longing to do them some good if they would but let you, but it is so difficult to get them to take up new ideas."[26] One of the many wonderful ironies of the novel will be that it is the natives who do some good for the English, who also need—and receive—some new ideas.

Bathurst is fortunately able to receive these on schedule: at the critical moment when Isobel would otherwise be captured and imprisoned at Kanpur (and then either murdered in the historical "slaughter" there or taken into the Nana Sahib's zenana), he confesses to Dr. Wade, the army surgeon, "I am afraid I am getting superstitious; but I feel as if Rujub knows of some danger impending and that he is somehow conveying that impression to me."[27] Of course this is the case, and between Rujub and Rabda, they will save the lovers' lives.

23. Ibid., 280.
24. Ibid., 310.
25. Ibid.
26. Ibid., 88.
27. Ibid., 298.

In the mutiny novel, key events are narrated again and again, and from novel to novel, and events that come to be remembered as key but which probably or certainly never happened, including many rapes, murders, and dismemberments, are also narrated repeatedly, taking on what Jenny Sharpe describes as the "truth effects of fiction."[28] At one juncture in the heated action of battle, the narrative of *Rujub* pauses, and we are suddenly given a list of casualties that have taken place over a period of weeks:

> Mr. Hunter, Captain Rintoul, and Richards had died of fever. Farquharson had been killed by a cannon ball; two civilians had been badly wounded; several of the children had succumbed; Amy Hunter had been killed by a shell that passed through a sandbag protection.[29]

It is as if these casualties are suddenly remembered, or if the *idea* of casualties is suddenly remembered. Oh yes, terrible fighting, we need some deaths here; a list ensues. Not everyone who dies is especially important—they don't all get proper names, but the fact of British "war dead" is important, and a long list is the necessary gesture of the genre.

As the truism has it, fiction is often used to make history legible. Arguing the reverse position, Ian Duncan describes what he calls Hume's "rationale for historical fiction":

> sketching in effect a rationale for historical fiction, Hume inverts the usual didactic ratio that makes fiction an agreeable vehicle for historical truth. Here history is the vehicle: the record of what is accepted as true helps accustom the reader, suspending their judgment, to the tropes of fiction. . . . History makes familiar—it provides the shared referential framework for—the figures of romance: a process

<hr>

28. Jenny Sharpe, *Allegories of Empire* (Minneapolis: University of Minnesota Press, 1993), 61.

29. Henty, *Rujub, or the Juggler*, 273.

that does not however, oblige readers to mistake romance for reality.[30]

It does not *oblige* readers to mistake romance for reality, but it does not *prohibit* them from doing so. History might provide a referential framework that *becomes* romance, or a flexibly referential framework that can become romance. Indeed, the mutiny was understood, as a writer in an 1897 *Blackwood's Edinburgh Magazine* essay wrote, to "provide every element of romance that could be desired in a story. Valour, heroism, cruelty and treachery, sharp agony and long endurance, satiated vengeance and bloodthirsty hatred."[31] The romance of the mutiny makes history available as fiction, as fact, as good yarn, as information, as a source for formulating beliefs about a not-too-distant war that deeply traumatized Britain's self-conception, in Christopher Herbert's problematic, but I think essentially correct assessment.[32]

The romance of history, the historical romance, the historical fiction produces "truth effects" that in turn produce a collective, if implicit "what if." This is not counterfactuality precisely, because the "what if" is not explicit, and the full exercise of what might have been is not carried out. It is simply gestured at vaguely, enough to offer events that may have occurred. Thus Nana Sahib may have said what we hear him to have said— perhaps someone even "reported" this conversation as Rujub

30. Ian Duncan, *Scott's Shadow: The Novel in Romantic Edinburgh* (Princeton, NJ: University Press, 2007), 128.

31. Hilda Gregg, "The Indian Mutiny in Fiction," *Blackwood's Edinburgh Magazine*, February 1897, 218–31, 219.

32. Herbert suggests that for many Victorians the "Indian Mutiny did mark a terrible break in history and the beginning of a dire new epoch . . . it was because it seemed to let out of it bottle a genie of fanatical cruelty impossible to reconcile with the Victorian creed of a world transformed by the progress of humanitarianism and 'civilization'" (*War of No Pity*, 133). I'm not sure where plantation slavery, the Opium Wars, the previous colonization of India, the settling of Australia, North America, and New Zealand fit in here, but perhaps Herbert is ventriloquizing Victorian self-assessments.

later "reports" conversations with the Rajah.[33] And perhaps Rujub's psychic abilities are also "real," and some day they will be explained by British psychology or neurology, as several British characters in the novel, like the army physician Dr. Wade, for example, believe.

Nana Sahib speaks and becomes contingent; the Kanpur slaughter is renarrated and becomes all the more definite; the heroine is saved by telepathy. The novel in general, and awkward subspecies of it like *Rujub the Juggler*, gives us many ontological and narrative spaces in which to think and even imagine our existences, and certainly those of characters, simultaneously. We have, in *Rujub the Juggler*, the domain of the historical, the domain of the fictional, and the domain of the occult or supernatural to inhabit. The world of the historical is rendered contingent by the fictionalizing of a historical character; the domain of fiction is rendered historical by the participation of its characters in historical events; the domain of the supernatural promises that knowing what has happened or will happen is a variable ability: Rujub can read the past and future in the smoke from the special powder that he sprinkles on fire; he can prevent the future from happening because he can see it coming. He actually has counterfactual agency: Isabel *will* be raped by the Nana Sahib, and/or she *will* be killed at Kanpur (although, very oddly, she is "based" on a historical character who was possibly raped but not killed, and who in fact married one of her Muslim captors), and Rujub sees this and arranges a different future for her. So history can be changed, the future can be colonized, but in this case by the colonized, and by a colonized subject who, however marginally, is on the side of the decolonizing rebels.

The novel also offers a world in which a deep level of sympathy obtains between British colonizers and Indian decolonizers: the narrator emphasizes that Rujub and Rabda could not communicate with Bathurst and Isobel otherwise. At the end

33. Henty, *Rujub, the Juggler*, 284.

of the novel, Isobel is back in England, wed to Ralph. The only "distinct messages" she receives from Rabda are by post and not by telepathy, but she still sometimes feels that Rabda is "with her."[34] The two exchange letters and gifts every year. The circuit of communication remains open at various levels of technical and psychic ability. In this way, the novel also generates a kind of heterodoxy—in regard to the possibility of supernatural experience and in regard to political and national sympathies—which would of course never have been Henty's conscious plan. Rather, the novel, in its generic drive to generate ontological multiplicity, imagines worlds that are possible if improbable, and in so doing, it may betray the tangle of beliefs that such worlds generate, some of which will, to quote Gauri Viswanathan, "bring the imagination into open conflict with pre-existing belief."[35] So the novel, for all of its tendency to produce worlds that allow us to disavow our one-worldly condition, also allows us to imagine worlds, in which we avoid a future that some people can read, whether or not all of us can see it.

Coda: Steerforth at Large

When a character called Forster sets out at a critical moment on a dangerous mission to seek help and supplies, Mrs. Doolan, a plain-spoken Irish character (most Irish characters in the nineteenth century speak plainly), remarks that "Steerforth's character might have been sketched from Forster. He is a man without heart or conscience."[36] This judgment turns out to be unfair, but that need not detain us here. If a historical character is, in Barthes's expert opinion, a superb reality effect, what about a fictional character from another diegetic universe? I would argue that Steerforth in *Rujub, the Juggler* is actually the supreme

34. Ibid., 385.

35. Gauri Viswanathan, "Secularism in the Frame of Heterodoxy," *PMLA* 123, no. 2 (March 2008): 472.

36. Henty, *Rujub, the Juggler*, 272.

reality effect, and the supreme fiction, at one and the same time. Steerforth can only enter Rujub inside of the diegesis of *David Copperfield*. He cannot be in any way contingent in the way that historical figures can become contingent or he will destabilize every world that the novel has established, collapsing all of them into a fictional *mis en abyme*. He is more insistently *referential* than a historical figure—"Steerforth" refers to an *actual character* in *David Copperfield*. A historical figure can become contingent, can enact counterfactuality, and yet not completely undermine the referentiality of every ontological level of a novel. But Steerforth can only enter *Rujub* in a secure, metalepsis-proof container: the diegetic world(s) of *David Copperfield*. So that the ruptures I am analyzing in this book have a limit, and that limit is the transit between fictional worlds: once that exchange happens, then reference is cancelled. Realism, what we think of as the realistic in fiction, requires reference to remain undecidable and unstable but always partly in touch with an intact world. As two child psychologists have shown, even small children understand that Batman knows that SpongeBob is not real. If Batman believes in SpongeBob, and, more importantly for our purposes, if they go out for coffee or play ping-pong together, there is no possibility for the discretionary practice of belief.[37] One can only disbelieve, and thoroughly. And belief, to return for a moment to Hume, is an activity that reading fiction produces.[38] Social life depends on it (we need to be able to imagine where we are not and whom we are not with), and fiction teaches us how to do it. The kind of ruptures different fictions provide teach us how to imagine the spaces of social life, and the possible histories to

37. See Deena Skolnick and Paul Bloom, "What Does Batman Think about SpongeBob?: Children's Understanding of the Fantasy/Fantasy Distinction," *Cognition* 101 (2006): 9–18.

38. "Hume's formal account of fiction takes shape around the topic of belief," Duncan argues, and he goes on to adumbrate the ways in which social life depends on the collective imagining of "the vital substance that gives body to a formal scheme" (*Scott's Shadow*, 128–29).

which we can subscribe, as we decide on fictionality and reference, case by case. But they also leave open the possibilities of hetero-ontologicality, in which various kinds of being and beings mingle and mix, allowing us to imagine future worlds and ways of living with ourselves and all of the others we have evicted from having and inhabiting "our own world."

Reference

WE ALL BELIEVE, in one way or another, in the agency, return, and presence of the dead. Whether it is in the form of history, the unconscious, mourning, melancholia, the commodity fetish, the heirloom, the will, the grave, or the family photo album, the dead clearly make meaning in and of our lives. We might call all of these beliefs continuous with the belief in ghosts that has been so difficult for various churches, the advent of "Enlightenment," and other forms of discipline to eradicate. It will be helpful to evince at least a temporary belief in ghosts for the duration of this chapter, because I am going to try to read them literally and denotatively in what follows, in order to suggest the virtues of forestalling allegory and rationalization that literal representations of the invisible or incredible tend to invite. Ghosts are for some of us literal and for some of us only allegorical: I want to think of them as both at once, in order to consider what I call "ghostly reference." Ghostly reference is a malleable aspect of representation, a formal nexus that allows for the free play of belief and the production of worlds—two necessary conditions for the formation and sustenance of the liberal subject, as I will discuss in what follows. Refusing to give up the ghost slows ghostly reference to a halt, allowing us to think about the materiality as well as the meaning of the ghost.

Primitive Ghosts and Allegorical Ghosts

Some ghosts are more literal than others in the history of Anglo-American literary criticism. Consider the ghosts of William Shakespeare and those of Amos Tutuola. When Tutuola "burst onto the postwar metropolitan literary scene" in 1952, with his novel *The Palm-Wine Drinkard*, it "provoked controversy for its episodic rendering of Yoruba folktales in nonstandard English."[1] These "folktales" consist of a narrative about an "expert," that is, a bottomless pit of a palm-wine drinker who ends up searching among the dead ("deads") for his dead palm-wine tapster. Published by Faber in London, the editors discussed the work at length to determine its authenticity, purity, and anthropological normativity. Indeed, the Faber editors had the work vetted by an anthropologist, Daryll Forde (a "specialist on Africa"), to make sure it was "authentic."[2] Selden Rodman, reviewing *The Palm-Wine Drinkard* in the *New York Times*, described Tutuola as a "true primitive."[3] Cid Corman, reviewing the 1954 Grove edition of Tutuola's second novel, *My Life in the Bush of Ghosts*, praises Tutuola's "colorful literal usages of language."[4] Tutuola's various spirits get taken literally—they are the stuff of a "primitive mind" retelling Yoruban folktales. Tutuola's ghosts, like those of Shakespeare, derive from folklore, literary sources, and Christianity.[5] A reader of the *Arabian Nights*, Lewis Carroll, and the Bible,

1. Gail Low, "The Natural Artist: Publishing Amos Tutuola's *The Palm-Wine Drinkard* in Postwar Britain," *Research in African Literatures* 37, no. 4 (Winter 2006): 15.

2. Ibid., 22.

3. Qtd. in ibid., 15. Selden Rodman, "Book Review of *Palm-Wine Drinkard*," *New York Times* Book Review, September 20, 1953.

4. Cid Corman, review of *My Life in the Bush of Ghosts*, by Amos Tutuola, *Books Abroad* 29, no. 1 (Winter 1955): 10.

5. Ato Quayson notes that "Christianity in Africa gave the realms of the supernatural a repulsive charm" (*Strategic Transformations in Nigerian Writing: Orality and History in the Work of Reverend Samuel Johnson, Amos Tutuola, Wole Soyinka, and Ben Okri* [Bloomington: Indiana University Press, 1997], 59).

Tutuola infuses his fiction with much that is not traditionally Yoruban: ghosts attend conferences and build colonial infrastructures with "Crown Agents" available for trade, missionary-style publishing houses provide printed matter, and one ghost sports television hands, on which the mortal, and deeply lost, narrator of *My Life in the Bush of Ghosts* can see what his family is doing back in the land of the living. British and American reviewers and readers nonetheless who read Tutuola's fiction purely as "African" could engage in the complex borrowing that is characteristic of primitivism, in which the belief of the other can be entertained for entertainment.

Tutuola's work was published in Britain and America (and shortly thereafter in Europe) at the same time that the phenomenon that Phil Ford describes as "exotica" was in full cultural swing. Featuring such various products as the jungle movie *Cobra Woman*, the "Mai Tai by the pool," Trader Vic's restaurant chain, Les Baxter's 1951 B movie-music-like LP *Ritual of the Savage*, exotica absorbs "the real into the imaginary and [erodes] . . . the boundaries between them. . . . Exotica is a spectacle of the real, to be consumed neither as a reality nor as a pure fantasy, but as some pleasurable, disquieting union of both."[6] There is no concern for authenticity or ethnographic representation in exotica, although there may be a "rhetoric of authenticity" at work in this cultural form.[7] This deeply middlebrow vein of widespread mid-century primitivism was perhaps a source of anxiety for the very highbrow Faber editors, who wanted to be sure that they were publishing a genuine, natural, authentic, and purely "African" text, which might also be consumed as a pleasurable and disquieting mix of reality and fantasy, of ethnography and folktale.[8]

6. Phil Ford, "Taboo: Time and Belief in Exotica," *Representations* 103, no. 1 (Summer 2008): 112.

7. Ibid., 113.

8. See Low's analysis of Tutuola's *Palm-Wine Drinkard* as a "Faber-artifact" in "The Natural Artist," 30ff.

As a paratextual authenticity effect, a facsimile page of Tutu-ola's handwritten manuscript was reproduced in the first edition, after a wonderful but eventually baseless scare to the effect that Tutuola had "employed a literary 'ghost' or 'ghosts' " to write out the manuscript.[9] Gail Low points out that this traditional signifier of literary value "functions as a signifier of an untampered and unedited (or lightly edited) childlike text written by a (then) unknown African." The book was "framed as an exotic artifact."[10] The facsimile page is captioned "A page from the author's MS. showing the publisher's 'corrections.' "[11] The scare quotes indicate that the corrections are actually something else: minimal edits to make the text legible, while still preserving what Dylan Thomas called its "young English."[12]

Tutuola's work was read literally for a long time because readers could believe in the authenticity of his belief. He was not constructing allegory, or symbolic fiction of any kind: his were simple tales, relating to the traditions of Yoruban narrative, infused with a spicy, still-African dash of colonial and Christian flavor. As an example of an African mind, his apparent beliefs and ideas were part of the value of his work in a way that Shakespeare's or Dickens's ghosts are not literally valued, or, for that matter, literally "read."[13]

Shakespeare's ghosts, also derived from folklore, literary sources, and Christianity, are rationalized and allegorized very

---

9. Alan Pringle to Geoffrey Parrinder, August 26, 1954; qtd. in ibid., 25.

10. Ibid.

11. Amos Tutuola, *The Palm-Wine Drinkard and My Life in the Bush of Ghosts* (New York: Grove Press, 1994), 208.

12. Dylan Thomas, "Blithe Spirits," *Observer*, July 6, 1952; repr., *Critical Perspectives on Amos Tutuola*, ed. Bernth Lindfors (New York: Lynne Rienner Publishers, 1975), 3.

13. See Achille Mbembe, "Life, Sovereignty, and Terror in the Fiction of Amos Tutuola," trans. R. R. Mitsch, *Research in African Literatures* 34, no. 4 (Winter 2003): 1. Ben Okri's claiming of Tutuola as a literary forebear was perhaps the beginning of Tutuola's literary legitimacy. Thanks to Susan Andrade for this point.

early in the project of Anglo-American literary criticism; beginning in the nineteenth century, "a preoccupation with psychological realism has led Shakespeare's admirers to avert their eyes from his contribution to what has come to be seen as a downmarket genre."[14] Elmer Edgar Stoll, a maverick early twentieth-century critic, took issue with this trend of "romantic" criticism to rationalize these ghosts,[15] which helped to transform Shakespeare from "a natural rather than a learned poet"[16] into Coleridge's "Genius."[17] Stoll insisted in a 1907 *PMLA* article that Shakespeare's ghosts are "objective": they are the "witches and wizards of James I, who ride on a broomstick and sail in a sieve, boil unspeakable caldrons, call up spirits and familiars, and raise storms."[18] In Shakespeare, Stoll insists, "all possibility of allegory . . . is foreclosed." "His portents and omens, his prophecies and soothsayings and presentiments, are of the same stripe. They are all literal, objective, binding."[19] Stoll is arguing against the kind of criticism in which ghosts must have a meaning beyond their folkloric or purgatorial connections; they must be figures rather than facts, literary (derived from

14. Catherine Belsey, "Shakespeare's Sad Tale for Winter: *Hamlet* and the Tradition of Fireside Ghost Stories," *Shakespeare Quarterly* 61, no. 1 (Spring 2010): 2. "Sources" of Shakespeare's ghosts continue to be debated and researched: see Catherine Belsey, *Why Shakespeare* (New York: Palgrave Macmillan, 2007); and "Shakespeare's Sad Tale for Winter," for folkloric sources; and Stephen Greenblatt, *Hamlet in Purgatory* (Princeton, NJ: Princeton University Press, 2001), for Catholic sources.

15. Elmer Edgar Stoll, "The Objectivity of Ghosts in Shakespeare," *PMLA* 22, no. 2 (1907): 201–33.

16. Hugh Grady, "Shakespeare Criticism, 1600–1900," in *Cambridge Companion to Shakespeare*, ed. Margareta de Grazia and Stanley Wells (Cambridge: Cambridge University Press, 2001), 266.

17. S. T. Coleridge, *Seven Lectures on Shakespeare and Milton* (London, 1856), viii, http://books.google.com/books?id=blru4BId2N8C&printsec =frontcover&dq=coleridge+AND+shakespeare&hl=en&sa=X&ei=8nsWUtLoGZb -4AP7w4CYAg&ved=0CEUQ6AEwBA#v=onepage&q=coleridge%20AND%20 shakespeare&f=false.

18. Stoll, "The Objectivity of Ghosts in Shakespeare," 230.

19. Ibid.

Seneca, for example) rather than literal. Perhaps not until Derrida's *Specters of Marx* do Shakespeare's ghosts again find such literal interpretation: "The one who says 'I am thy father's spirit' can only be taken at his word."[20] In general, though, we haven't taken Hamlet's father at his word, and we have asked much more about what Shakespeare's ghosts *mean* than what they *are*. Even in New Historicist accounts as different as those of Catherine Belsey and Stephen Greenblatt, in which ghosts are, respectively, traced to folklore and to purgatory, the materiality of the ghost dissolves into textuality and figuration.[21] In contrast to Tutuola's ghosts, Shakespeare's ghosts have been, even in materialist approaches, allegorized thoroughly and irretrievably, rationalized to the point that we lose contact with the beliefs that preceded the banishing of ghosts from the realm of the "rational" in the seventeenth century. Here metaphor and meaning replace the living dead in whom Elizabethans routinely believed, despite the banishing of purgatory by the Protestant church; we do not explore the heterodoxy at the heart of our canon, the set of beliefs that make our "greatest" writers completely unlike us, and perhaps unbearably so. The footnotes in any Shakespeare edition may refer to folklore and other source material for ghosts and fairies and other supernatural phenomena, but the assumption is that Shakespeare has transformed—translated—this material from the literal to the figural. He is the individual genius rather than the tribal medium, the intentional author rather than the communal mind saturated with untransformed legend.

Tutuola and Shakespeare are emblems of two problems in literary critical reading: *literal* reading of a text that is assumed itself to be only literal and *allegorical* reading of a text that is itself assumed to be only allegorical. Critical theory, especially postcolonial theory, has retrieved Tutuola's texts from their

20. Jacques Derrida, *Specters of Marx: The State of Debt, the Work of Mourning, and the New International*, trans. Peggy Kamuf (New York: Routledge, 1994), 7.

21. See Belsey, *Why Shakespeare*; and Greenblatt, *Hamlet in Purgatory*.

rigidly literal fate; literal and denotative reading must retrieve Shakespeare and the rest of our meaningful, symbolical, intentional, literary, individually written texts from their rigidly allegorical fate. The literal and denotative in Shakespeare is in the footnotes, quite literally: there we find folklore and the Elizabethan object world, issues of Christian belief and the meanings of archaic words. But definition is not enough; we must do the interpretive work that much denotation actually requires, as Cannon Schmitt's work on Joseph Conrad and Robert Louis Stevenson so wonderfully demonstrates.[22] Tutuola's text is published without annotation (to this day): it, apparently, coincides with itself. As an early critic observed, he believed that the spirit world was contiguous with our own. Interestingly, the "rational" view is that the spirits live in some other world—heaven or hell. Ghosts offer us the possibility of flexing our belief systems, and imagining "worlds." The primitive, the genuine African lives in one world; the liberal subject, on the other hand, requires many, in part to disavow the many death-worlds that can be variously construed, in the flexing of the genre, as reality or fantasy, history or fiction, as rupturing diegetic and ontological levels break the world into worlds. "We must be careful not to reify belief," Jean-Claude Schmitt warns us, "to turn it into something established once and for all, something that individuals and societies need only express and pass on to each other."[23]

Unserious Ghosts

There is a context that might be said to fall between Shakespeare and Tutuola, and not just in temporal terms, one in which we

22. See Cannon Schmitt, "Tidal Conrad (Literally)," *Victorian Studies* 55, no. 1 (Autumn 2012): 7–29; and "Technical Maturity in Robert Louis Stevenson," *Representations* 125, no. 1 (Winter 2014): 54–79.

23. Jean-Claude Schmitt, *Ghosts in the Middle Ages: The Living and the Dead in Medieval Society*, trans. Teresa Lavender Fagan (Chicago: University of Chicago Press, 1998), 7.

can try ghosts on in a semifamiliar, domesticated, kind of silly belief system. This is the Victorian ghost story. We can dismiss these stories and laugh at them the way we laugh at the weird aspects of our own cultural past. We can't really take them literally: white, British, literate people from a century and a half ago are not regarded as "primitive," despite their commonalities with other people so classed. And yet, it is hard to take them figuratively: their ghosts do not resolve into "meaning" very well; they are not "haunting" in the way that Hamlet's father or Tutuola's television-handed ghost stay with us long after we are finished reading.

This may be because, although many Victorians believed in ghosts, Victorian ghost stories don't tend to. Or, more precisely, they refuse to settle the issue of belief. Their titles are ambivalent or anxious or defensive—"To be Taken with a Grain of Salt," "Reality or Delusion," "The Truth, the Whole Truth, and Nothing but the Truth," "The Man of Science."[24] There is almost always a narrative disavowal. In Dinah Mulock's "The Last House in C___ Street," the narrator declares in the story's first two sentences, "I am not a believer in ghosts in general. I see no good in them."[25] A believable ghost story follows—that is to say, one with compelling evidence of the existence of a ghost. So part of the formula is a beginning statement by a narrator or character in which there is a flat declaration along the lines of "I don't believe in ghosts, or I didn't believe in ghosts until I met the one in the story I'm about to tell you." Julia Briggs notes that, unlike the gothic, and unlike the detective story, the ghost story does not resolve its own mystery, the ghost.[26] This would seem to leave the interpretive field wide open, and yet the ghost story is very

24. *The Oxford Book of Victorian Ghost Stories*, ed. Michael Cox and R. A. Gilbert (Oxford: Oxford University Press, 2003).

25. Dinah Mulock, "The Last House in C___ Street," in Cox and Gilbert, *The Oxford Book of Victorian Ghost Stories*, 44.

26. Julia Briggs, *Night Visitors: The Rise and Fall of the English Ghost Story* (London: Faber, 1977), 11.

little attended to, especially if we consider it in comparison with its contemporary, the much-analyzed detective story. Srdjan Smajic notes that we are as likely to see a ghost as we are to see "new scholarship on the subject."[27] Yet ghost stories are important to the Victorian period: taking off in periodicals between 1830 and 1850, they peak in the two decades between 1870 and 1890 and peter out rapidly in the opening decades of the twentieth century. They were written by everyone: Charles Dickens, Mary Elizabeth Braddon, Wilkie Collins, Margaret Oliphant, Elizabeth Gaskell, Rhoda Broughton, Amelia Edwards, Vernon Lee, Henry James, and M. R. James: the genre was deeply attractive to writers across a wide spectrum of high-, middle-, and lowbrow authors.

The lack of critical attention to the ghost story may have to do with the apparent anomaly of the ghost story itself. If the dominant mode of Victorian fiction—realism—relies on visibility, legibility, and thoroughgoing epistemological closure, the ghost story questions the evidence of sight, the possibility of reading that evidence accurately.[28] More important, it refuses to decide on whether or not we can truly "be in touch with those we cannot touch" (in Francis O'Gorman's memorable phrase).[29] The "ghost" problem is not solved: we are left with two distinct ontological realms at the end of the ghost story: the one in which ghosts do exist and the one in which they do not. We inhabit that ruptured space, and so do many characters who do not know what they have seen, or if what they have heard of what someone else has seen is true. The ghost story is metaleptically ruptured by the intrusion of belief into disbelief, and of disbelief into

27. Srdjan Smajic, *Ghost-Seers, Detectives, and Spiritualists: Theories of Vision in Victorian Literature and Science* (Cambridge: Cambridge University Press, 2010), 11.

28. For a thorough analysis of Victorian visuality, ghost seeing, and ghost fiction, see ibid.

29. Francis O'Gorman, "What Is Haunting Tennyson's *Maud* (1855)?," *Victorian Poetry* 48, no. 3 (Fall 2010): 298.

belief. There is a kind of play between these two levels, a heterotopia for which no resolution is offered, or even attempted. I want to argue that this metaleptic fracture emblematic of the ghost story is actually similar to the dominant realist mode. It is not an anomaly; rather, it is a feature of fiction that realism tried and tries to naturalize. That is to say, the realist novel wants to refer to real people, events, and places, yet it also wants to distribute lots of fictional people, things, and places among that real stuff, creating a seemingly seamless integration of two very different diegetic and ontological worlds. We don't feel a sense of rupture or uncanniness when we think of the fictional characters who inhabit actual cities or when we think of actual wars interrupting or furthering fictional plot. I argue here that we should.

According to a literary critical orthodoxy that took hold in the late 1970s, the nineteenth-century, and in Britain, the specifically Victorian novel, eschews the typical self-mocking and/ or self-conscious apparatuses of eighteenth-century, modernist, and postmodern novels. And yet Victorian writers also produce the largest form of metaleptic rupture those self-undermining fictions point out in themselves: the problem that two ontological levels—the fictional and the referential—must coexist and cannot be melded together. When Jane Eyre apostrophizes the reader about her marriage, when the American Civil War interrupts a conversation in *Daniel Deronda*, when Pip walks by Smithfield Market, these fictions also produce the metaleptic ruptures of *Tristram Shandy*'s plot diagrams or Mark Z. Danielewski's footnotes to footnotes in *House of Leaves*. The ghost story, like other fictions that cannot bring representation and the world represented into alignment, epitomizes and indeed emphasizes this problem—if it is a problem.

What seems like a kind of narrative dislocation, lack of resolution, or epistemological crisis might also be viewed as the perfect liberal narrative form. It is no mistake that clerks, men of science, Scrooges, "materialists," and other unsentimental and determinedly nonspiritual types are often the hosts of ghosts. These are rational people who must decide, and allow us to decide, based on their experience, what to believe. This is the ultimate liberal experience as described by Elaine Hadley in *Living Liberalism*: the point of liberal cognition is to have private, apparently self-generated opinions. We think what we choose to think, each by each. Interestingly, the liberal individual is also something of a ghost herself:

> In place of the brutal social body, riven by violent divisions of interest; in place of the vulgar classed body, burdened by impulses and habits; even in place of the physical body, determined by its biology, mid-Victorian liberalism offers the promise of abstracted individuality.[30]

Hadley puts it in even more precisely spectral terms: "The liberal citizen [of the mid-Victorian period] is an heir of . . . ghosts that haunt the civic sphere of liberal discourse."[31] In Locke's *Two Treatises on Government* (which Hadley goes on to quote), the executive of the commonwealth "has no right to obedience, nor can claim it otherwise than as the public person invested with the power of the law; and so is to be considered as the image, phantom, or representative of the commonwealth, acted by the will of society, declared in its laws; and thus he has no will, no power, but that of the law."[32] The leader of liberal citizens leads only as long as he is haunted by the law, and must be obeyed not as a person but as an image of, or a phantom representing, the law.

The liberal citizen and its leaders are ghostly because they must be capable of an abstracted, formalized, and spiritualized disembodiment. The rational is constituted by this seemingly other realm of thought and feeling: a realm of spirits, of the

30. Elaine Hadley, *Living Liberalism: Practical Citizenship in Mid-Victorian Britain* (Chicago: University of Chicago Press, 2010), 64.

31. Ibid., 59–60n41.

32. John Locke, Two Treatises of Government *and* A Letter Concerning Toleration, ed. Ian Shapiro (New Haven, CT: Yale University Press, 2003), 167.

insubstantial, of the invisible. The visible world and the invisible world coexist in liberal thinking because one world is not enough. There is the escape hatch, the open circuit, of the alternative world, the possibility of embodiment for the disembodied, of disembodiment for the embodied. Your best self is the self in your disembodied mind; the equally necessary but less elevated self is the consuming, desiring, reproductive, social self, the one that is embodied. So the ghost in the Victorian ghost story might function as the individual who is in some sense both present and absent, physical and immaterial.

The ghost is linked to that individual from another direction: that of purgatory. Purgatory was "invented" in response to the pressure of popular belief in ghosts, a category the early church had disposed of, completely unsuccessfully, just as, centuries later, "the Protestant abolition of purgatory made very little impact on [the] popular custom" of believing in ghosts.[33] Jean-Claude Schmitt, in his history of ghosts in the Middle Ages, contends that ghost stories rise in the twelfth century with the Mendicant tradition of preaching in which monks became reliant on individuals rather than on aristocratic families.[34] In the aristocratic tradition, it was up to the families of the dead to leave monks land as recompense for saying prayers for the souls of the dead. In the Mendicant tradition, individuals in their wills left money to monks to say a certain number of masses to lessen their time in purgatory, ushering in what Jacques Chiffoleau calls the "accounting of the hereafter."[35] "Ghost tales," Schmitt writes, "reinforced the economic implications of penance."[36] Ghosts, in short, are bourgeois.

Hadley's liberal individual endlessly working out opinions and beliefs and Chiffoleau's bookkeeping into the beyond

33. Belsey, "Shakespeare's Sad Tale for Winter," 9.
34. Schmitt, *Ghosts in the Middle Ages*.
35. Qtd. in ibid., 142.
36. Ibid., 126.

suggest problems with recording data, or with the need to separate data from connotation. We need what we think of as denotation: transparent designation. The interpretable must be in a separate category of language from information, or else a system in which books and records can be kept is impossible. In a crucial moment of Franco Moretti's *The Bourgeois*, he asks, a propos of a particularly, and mind-bogglingly, detailed passage from *Middlemarch*, "What has made precision so much more important than meaning?"[37] My question is, rather, what has delinked precision from meaning, or more precisely, from meaning beyond definition?[38] Moretti moves in the next paragraph to what Goethe, in *Wilhelm Meister's Apprenticeship*, calls the "beauty" of double-entry bookkeeping. That is the answer to both his question and my own, of course. The "precision" of bookkeeping in two columns can only be beautiful if both columns are exempt from the exfoliations of connotative meaning, and from the (multiple) interpretations that will produce it. Denotation must be that which ends with a definition, a deictic "this is that." When we say, as we often do, that *Middlemarch* is "encyclopedic," we don't really mean it. If we did, we would understand that to interpret it requires expanding on it, not shrinking it. "Reading" *Middlemarch* means reading the Vatican art, the stethoscopes, the emeralds, the muslin, the poaching, the plans for cottages, the meaning of Polish-ness, fever, both of the first two Reform Bills, Saint Teresa, the epic, the epigraph, the novel, and the stuff in Casaubon's pigeon holes, and the system of pigeon holes themselves. Just as a beginning. If lists have meaning, our labor will have to be decommodified and unalienated, because it will be endless. Any kind of mastery will

37. Franco Moretti, *The Bourgeois: Between History and Literature* (London: Verso, 2013), 85.

38. In my book *The Ideas in Things: Fugitive Meaning in the Victorian Novel* (Chicago: University of Chicago Press, 2006), I tried to bring them together.

be hopeless. Readings will be absolutely temporary and obviously makeshift.

Jury Duty

In the Victorian ghost story, the ghost is often—I would say usually—a collectively experienced "appearance," as Dickens calls one murdered returnee in the story "To Be Taken with a Grain of Salt" (1865). The narrator reads an account of a murder in a newspaper and immediately "sees" the scene in "a flash—rush— flow . . . like a picture impossibly painted on a moving river."[39] He is only relieved not to see the dead body in it. He gets up to look out the window to clear his head, and sees murderer and murderee ghost-walking through Picadilly. Anyone who touches the narrator also becomes haunted by the case. By a lively coincidence, the narrator (whose name we never learn, and who will not give the names involved in the murder case but—in the kind of documentary effect typical of these tales—does give the "real" name of his servant) is called for jury duty and ends up as the foreman on the very case that has been haunting him. The ghost of the murdered man is constantly in court, trying to direct the evidence toward conviction of the accused murderer. And it is no mistake that this story is to be taken with a grain of salt, because there are actually two ghosts, or two hauntings in it, and one of the ghosts is still alive. When the murderer is convicted, his last words before the sentence of death is pronounced are, "My Lord, I knew I was a doomed man when the Foreman of my Jury came into the box. My Lord, I knew he would never let me off, because, before I was taken, he somehow got to my bedside in the night, woke me, and put a rope round my neck."[40] The accused here reveals that he has been haunted by the jury

---

39. Charles Dickens, "To Be Taken with a Grain of Salt," *All the Year Round*, December 30, 1865, 34.
    40. Ibid., 37–38.

foreman for the entirety of the case. But what's curious about the ending of this story is that it comes after the information that "in the leading newspapers the following day" the convicted man's final speech was reported as "a few rambling, incoherent, and half-audible words, in which he was understood to complain that he had not had a fair trial because the Foreman of the Jury was prepossessed against him."[41] This weirdly "verifies" the haunting of the foreman; he *was pre*-possessed by the case. But what's interesting is that the murderer's words were not incoherent or half-audible to *everyone*, because the narrator reports them precisely, and they end the story—there is no comment on them or qualification of their exactness. So the indication seems to be that the leading newspapers cannot report the inexplicable, the empirically unverifiable, the possibly supernatural.

We don't routinely believe in ghosts because they aren't a part of the order of things in our world, the story seems to suggest: they aren't part of the iterable in factual discourse, especially perhaps in a court of law, although this court of law is "rationalized" by the supernatural; justice is done because of the careful directions to the jury of one ghost, and perhaps the emotional impact of another on the accused. Fiction is the space in which this kind of experience can be reported: it is the space in which belief and unbelief can coexist, or in which believing is a process rather than an accomplished creed, and in which readers and characters can maintain radical ontological flexibility. Simon During asks,

> Why is the technique for identifying supernatural fictions as fictions linked officially to skepticism? The answer is that, from about 1700, in general terms fiction was harnessed to the pedagogy of Enlightenment; furthermore, the enlightened consensus is that the empire of disbelief should colonize the territories of faith and fanaticism. To parse the skills

41. Charles Dickens, "Remarkable Confession of the Murderer," in *Christmas Stories from "Household Words" and "All The Year Round" and Other Stories* (London: Chapman and Hall, 1891), 311.

required to read supernatural fictions . . . is to increase the suppleness, agency and scope of disbelief itself.[42]

I would add that it is the *practice* of disbelief that is important, the formation and reformation of opinion in what Hadley calls "standardized . . . practices of cognitive individuation."[43] The narrator of "Grain of Salt" twice declines to offer what he describes as any "theory." The story will not explain the contagious, transitive, collective haunting by a ghost who melts away once his murderer is convicted. And this is absolutely conventional in the endings of ghost stories: Amelia Edwards's "Was It an Illusion?" for example, ends with the titular question repeated, unanswered. It is up to the reader to try on various beliefs and form an opinion. As Hadley has argued in an analysis of Anthony Trollope's *The Warden*, the opinion itself doesn't matter; "what counts is the form these opinions take."[44] And the activity of forming them, I would add.

So the ghostly referent is an injustice, an unpunished crime, and the crime in the ghost story usually is a murder, that most domestic and individual crime, and it must be avenged for the ghost to return to his or her proper sphere (wherever that is— perhaps it is part of our sphere, perhaps not). But what is interesting about the genre is that the ghost is often easily appeased, or the crime is readily available for understanding. And this is the thing: the ghost is explained, but the mystery of its existence is not solved. We know why there is a ghost, but we don't know if there is a ghost. This is a strange state of affairs. In other words, there's a good reason for a ghost to be present in the ghost story, but what is a ghost, and does it exist? Those questions are left to the side. And there was a large dual discourse in the same periodicals in which these tales were published both supporting the

42. Simon During, *Modern Enchantments: The Cultural Power of Secular Magic* (Cambridge, MA: Harvard University Press, 2002), 50.
43. Hadley, *Living Liberalism*, 65.
44. Ibid., 81.

existence of ghosts and "unveiling" or debunking various cases of ghost siting or hearing. The play of unbelief that the reader can experience in reading ghost stories continues outside them in apparently learned or responsible discursive spaces in which the matter is debated, and no resolution is possible. It turns out to be an issue of individual opinion, solidified as belief—which can be put back into play as the activity of wondering what to believe in the next story, the next "proof" of the existence of ghosts, or the next debunking.

Ghostly reference has another, perhaps larger function: it occurs wherever disavowal admits guilt into a discourse only to render it immaterial: unbelievable, inexplicable, and finally impossible to pursue logically, rationally, or scientifically. In this, ghostly reference promises relief from meaning, from guilt, and from the burden of history that it avows and then displaces onto the apparitional, a category that is never resolved. Ghostly reference offers us a form of endlessly shifting semiotic play: the play of reference, the play of meaning, and the play of belief each shield one another from any final resolution. We do not have to finally or fully believe in the ghost, or the history, that haunts it. Perhaps a more principled ghostbusting would, in general, involve taking literal ghosts figuratively and figurative ghosts literally.

Believing in the Ghosts of Others

In the United States in 1890, President Benjamin Harrison directed the secretary of war to conduct the largest military operation since the Civil War against the Sioux people because they were engaging, en masse, in the Ghost Dance, a ceremony the goal of which was to bring back from the dead their ancestors, at which point white people would be magically removed from the land. The historian Jeffrey Ostler points out the logical slips in the presidential thinking at the time: in order for the Sioux to effect the disappearance of white people, their ancestors would have to come back to life, a possibility presumably not entertained by the US government in the late nineteenth century.[45] The result of the government's fear of a dance that beckoned ghosts to return to earth was the slaughter at Wounded Knee. Perhaps the US government, like the murderer and the jury foreman in "To Be Taken with a Grain of Salt," was transitively haunted: as the Sioux were haunted by their ancestors, so the government was haunted by the Sioux. The desire for, or fear of, the dead occupying a literal place among the living creates a violent heterotope, the dystopian side of the liberal narrative in which ontological choice allows for individualized accounts of history, and eminent and imminent domain in multiple imaginary, and then often actual, spheres. This heterotope has been voraciously resolved by "removals": of native and indigenous peoples, Africans, and Irish and Scottish peoples in the way of English land-taking. Ghosts are outlawed at such moments. But they always return: as farce, as tragedy, as religion, and as an exercise in choosing what to believe, and more radically perhaps, what to see. After all, the ghost, as Dorothy Scarborough suggests, "is the really permanent citizen of this earth, for mortals, at best, are but transients."[46]

On the one hand, the detective story, like the mainstream of Victorian fiction, seems to resolve the world for us into legible people, places, and events; on the other hand, the ghost story makes all resolutions optional. Detective stories end with crimes solved: clues are "read," the guilty are apprehended, the case is turned over to the police. Ghost stories narrate the punishment of the guilty. They suggest that we are all haunted by the law, finally, and that justice will be done. At the same time, we live in a kind of purgatory, with the unquiet dead among us, reminding us of the useful instability of our diegetic and ontological habitations. This footloose transdiegetic travel forms a

45. Jeffrey Ostler, *The Plains Sioux and U.S. Colonialism: From Lewis and Clark to Wounded Knee* (Cambridge: Cambridge University Press, 2004).

46. Dorothy Scarborough, *The Supernatural in Modern English Fiction* (New York: G. P. Putnam's Sons, 1917), 81.

kind of haunting obverse metaphor for the literal instability of habitation of Tutuola's "deads" and ghosts, and for the Sioux who would not give up the ghost. Liberal subjects are at home everywhere and anywhere; subjects outside this formation are homeless, consigned to live "life in a fleeting mode," in which not only place but "particular being"—human or animal, dead or alive—is temporary.[47] That is perhaps one of the consequences of liberal freedom, and one of the consequences of liberal individualism, which has always been available only in very limited, and local, supply.

47. Mbembe, "Life, Sovereignty, and Terror," 19.

Decolonizing the Novel

IN HIS INTRODUCTION to Kōjin Karatani's *Origins of Modern Japanese Literature*, Fredric Jameson writes that the "raw material of Japanese social experience and the abstract formal patterns of Western novel construction cannot always be welded together seamlessly."[1] It is worth noting Jameson's use of the phrase "raw material" to refer to Japanese social life. It is as if the "abstract formal patterns of Western novel construction" roam the earth, and random non-Western authors try desperately to squish their experience into these (superior) formal patterns, desperate to produce a real novel.

This phrasing requires us to think about literary raw material, which is, after all, the stuff of the literary primitive accumulation that precedes the novel. In this case, it is a primitive accumulation that we like to think we don't need: we cannot put it to Western use, Jameson implies, unlike so many other raw materials of the "periphery." Curiously, Franco Moretti, in *Atlas of the European Novel*, also uses the term "raw material" when he claims that "bad literature is the raw material of literary

---

1. Fredric Jameson, introduction to *Origins of Modern Japanese Literature*, by Kōjin Karatani, trans. Brett de Bary (Durham, NC: Duke University Press, 1993), xiii.

evolution."[2] And yet we might just as easily reverse this formulation using the work of Srinivas Aravamudan, who has argued that the novel of the West rose due to a healthy extraction of raw material in the form of Oriental and Orientalist forms (not that I consider this "bad literature").[3] Macarena Gómez-Barris has written that "before the colonial project could prosper, it had to render territories and peoples extractable, and it did so through a matrix of symbolic, physical and representational violence."[4] Gómez-Barris writes about environmental destruction, but when she refers here to the symbolic and the representational, it is impossible not to think of the "great" nineteenth-century novels that took their raw materials from colonized places in so many registers: physically, in terms of the extraction of materials to make paper and ink, in earning money to pay for writing and publishing; linguistically, in terms of the barrage of loan words from Zulu, Hindi, Urdu, various Creoles and Pidgins, and so on, that populate the novel to give them "local" color, and in terms of the things that populate novels and make them seem "real" or "realistic," that derive directly from colonial extraction: tea, ivory, muslin, emeralds, sugar, tobacco, and so on: my list might be finite, but I don't know the end of it.[5]

This is actually very good news if we are going to try to decolonize the novel, a form that seems imprisoned in imperial and racial formations that we would quail at in other contexts. That is to say, our imagining of the novel has been inflected and infected by a racism that is somehow invisible to most observers. Many "non-Western" novel theorists have shown us new abstract formal patterns of the novel that are used either to ignore the

2. Franco Moretti, *Atlas of the European Novel, 1800–1900* (New York: Verso, 1999), 149.

3. See Srinivas Aravamudan, *Enlightenment Orientalism: Resisting the Rise of the Novel* (Chicago: University of Chicago Press, 2011).

4. Macarena Gómez-Barris, *The Extractive Zone: Social Ecologies and Decolonial Perspectives* (Durham, NC: Duke University Press, 2017), 5.

5. See Elaine Freedgood, *The Ideas in Things: Fugitive Meaning in the Victorian Novel* (Chicago: University of Chicago Press, 2006).

Western novel, or for innovative purposes that may or may not have any reference to the Western novel: "If 'world literature,'" as Francesca Orsini writes, "spurs all of us to consider wider trajectories of production, circulation, and recognition, why does it so often get the rest of the world wrong? And why does it seem to imprison non-Western literatures in categories, timelines, and explanations that do not fit?"[6]

That's the thing about the novel: it's not a pantoum or a sonnet; it's a form that accommodates and indeed thrives, for us as critics, on the very thing we most delight in finding: radical formal change. We have appreciated formal change readily and with marked consensus in "Western" novel history, but somehow when it happens in Japan or Nigeria or Brazil, it's not an innovation but a defect. It's not post-Western or post-anything: it's premodern and problematic. Andrew Goldstone makes the case for this in an excellent article on G. V. Desani's highly innovative *H. Hatterr*, arguing that works like Desani's require a "broker," who "not only converts an author's work in to the international currency of literary value, but is essential to the way that new capital generates interest."[7] In the case of Desani, as in that of the Nigerian novelist Amos Tutuola, T. S. Eliot became that "broker."[8] This suggests the kind of clout that one needs (major writer and major editor in one) to attain literary value under Western eyes.

Moretti famously takes up Jameson's assessment of the peripheral novel in his influential essay "Conjectures on World Literatures" and decides to "prove" as a "law" Jameson's idea of the underdevelopment of the "peripheral novel."[9] Moretti reads

6. Francesca Orsini, "The Multilingual Local in World Literature," *Comparative Literature* 67, no. 4 (2015): 370.

7. Andrew Goldstone, "Hatterr Abroad: G. V. Desani on the Stage of World Literature," *Contemporary Literature* 55, no. 3 (Fall 2014): 466–500.

8. See Elaine Freedgood, "Literary Debt," *PMLA* 131, no. 5 (October 2016): 1480–88.

9. Franco Moretti, "Conjectures on World Literature," *New Left Review* 1 (January–February 2000): 58.

the non-Western novel at an acknowledged distance; instead of reading these novels himself, he turns to novel theorists who read novels from outside the West to prove that they agree that their novels are not "seamless." I have tried to argue throughout this book that that there are no novels that are "seamless" and that such a condition is a dream of Western criticism, which, at a certain point, wants the novel to be great, invents realism, and makes it seem formally coherent. This happens first in France, as Margaret Cohen has shown, and then about 150 years later in Britain: "Before 1830, the novel in France was 'pleasant entertainment for lazy gentlefolk,' to cite the noted critic, Charles-Marie de Féletz. . . . After 1830, the genre became an authoritative form of social and cultural analysis imbued with the highest literary prestige."[10] Critics in the Victorian period often bewail the fact that British novel is not like the French novel (it is, for over a century, "peripheral" to it aesthetically—largely due to its length).

The dominant "world literature" model (Moretti, Damrosch, Jameson) requires an ideal British and French novel: smoothly realistic, one with no intrusive narrators or borrowings from other cultures, one that depicts social reality without too many hiccups or too much humbug. This is an extremely small Europe, as Sonia Werner has argued in her study "Fringe Realisms," which concerns not the global south but the fringes of Western Europe:

> In contrast to conventional definitions of realism, which identify its emergence with the rise of the novel in the modern, industrialized nation-states of France and England, *Fringe Realisms* examines overlooked bodies of realist literature that materialized contemporaneously in so-called belated nations such as Germany, Russia, and Italy. . . . I use the term "fringe realisms" to emphasize the ways in which such

10. Margaret Cohen, *The Sentimental Education of the Novel* (Princeton, NJ: Princeton University Press, 1999), 3.

movements depart from conventions associated with canonical realist prose. Instead of conceiving of these literatures as flawed derivatives of French and English models, the project offers an account of the inventive stylistic dimensions of other realist genres, including the novella, the chronicle, and the physiological sketch, to explore how such narrative forms produced different realities and reality effects.[11]

But, as I've tried to show in the introduction and the case studies, this "Western" (really British and French) novel doesn't exist. Therefore the so-called periphery of noveldom can no longer be accused of failing to adjust to novel "form." Indeed, the very idea of the periphery becomes more absurd than ever: literary form is assigned, not discovered, and novel form is infinitely adaptable (or we might say, findable). Moretti quotes Roberto Schwarz to the effect that outside Europe we find mostly "half-baked" literature.[12] And yet critics from the Victorian period through the Cold War regularly found many of our most canonical nineteenth-century novels half-baked: Dorothy Van Ghent counts as failures novels like *Vanity Fair*, and Barbara Hardy struggles to find aesthetic parity between Henry James and the then-peripheral George Eliot.[13] "Half-baked" might describe novel form in general, in fact: it is a term I can imagine Bakhtin approving: there is always something that can be added to the mix of languages and conventions that we call the novel. The Turkish critic Jale Parla has pointed out (to no avail apparently among critics outside Turkish literature) that "the instability of narrative voice cannot be confined to the rise of the novel in the third world, it was very much there in the rise of the novel in England and France as well."[14] Exactly.

11. Sonie Werner, Fringe Realisms: Literarature, Nation, and the Invention of a Usable Present" (PhD diss., New York University, 2016), iv.

12. Moretti, *Atlas of the European Novel, 1800–1900*, 195.

13. See introduction.

14. Jale Parla, "The Object of Comparison," *Comparative Literature Studies* 41, no. 1 (2004): 121.

If we can dislodge the aesthetic racism that has placed the British and French nineteenth-century novel at the masterful, still center of a novel history that is as contingent as the genre it tries to track, other novels might have a better chance of getting a reading that is not nineteenth-century-Anglo-Eurocentric. National or ethnic novel traditions might not be asked to follow the trajectory of a novel history that often demands a punctual arrival at and departure from realism before modernist or post-modernist "innovation" can be recognized as such. This version of novel history casts a menacing shadow: writing about the Turkish novel, for example, Ahmet O. Evin points out that "real-ism became not only an ideal to be pursued but at the same time the standard against which prose fiction would be judged."[15] Numerous national, linguistic, or ethnic surveys of novels from the periphery—Yiddish, Arabic, Turkish, and Chinese—often abase themselves before a modernity that they somehow can't catch up with: Matti Moosa, for example, contends that Ara-bic fiction is still involved with the Arabian Nights. (Whose fic-tion is not? This text continues to loom large over every form of fictional narrative, as Saree Makdisi and Felicity Nussbaum have thoroughly documented.)[16] Moosa apologizes for this "imi-tative" quality of the Arabic novel, but as Shaden M. Tageldin points out, there is a serious missing political link in much of the discussion of "world literature": "French colonialism and its imperial afterlives rewrote Egyptian self-understanding on the ground of the linguistic and the literary."[17] We cannot disen-tangle one literature from another in national terms, since impe-rialism has had a two-way effect on narrative: peripheral forms creep in, metropolitan forms creep out; national borders are

15. Ahmet O. Evin, *Origins and Development of the Turkish Novel* (Minne-apolis: Bibliotheca Islamica, 1983), 19.

16. See Saree Makdisi and Felicity Nussbaum, *The Arabian Nights in His-torical Context: Between East and West* (Oxford: Oxford University Press, 2008).

17. Shaden M. Tageldin, *Disarming Words: Empire and the Seduction of Translation in Egypt* (Berkeley: University of California Press, 2011), 108.

hard to maintain, as imperialism, colonialism, and all its massive social, political, and psychological effects have made such
circulation inevitable. In general, the seemingly neutral and
apolitical analyses of many current participants in the "World
Literature" scene belie the most obvious point: you can't mine
what Moretti calls "data" from critics of the periphery without
thinking deeply about where and how their thinking about the
novel developed. What Tageldin points out about the French
colonization of Arab "self-understanding" is also a feature of
theorists as diverse as Frantz Fanon thinking about the Antilles
and Gauri Viswanathan writing on colonial India.[18] Both have
demonstrated the ways in which literary and cultural forms
are subjectively transformative to colonized people: think of
Macauley's dream of turning South Asians into "Brown Brit-
ains" via literary study of British texts. But of course we have
the criticism of the last thirty years at least—from critical race
theory, postcolonial studies, psychoanalysis, Marxism, and
poststructuralism in general—that ought to undermine any
possibility of the dream of neutral data in literary criticism. But
criticism, as I noted in the introduction, is nothing if not forgetful of itself.

It is actually pretty simple to transform our reading practices
of the realist novel: instead of writing off British and French formal breakdowns as "anomalies," we could read them as constitu-
tive of messy, mostly hastily written novels that have been transformed by critics into polished forms. In the case studies in this
book, I deploy reading methods that we can commonly find in
criticism of the eighteenth-century novel, as well as the modernist and postmodernist novel. We can read paratexts as reflexive
in a way we don't now (because we scarcely read—that is to say

18. See Frantz Fanon, *Black Skin, White Masks*, trans. Richard Philcox (New
York: Grove Press, 2008); and Gauri Viswanathan, *Masks of Conquest: Literary
Study and British Rule in India* (New York: Columbia University Press, 2014).

interpret—them at all). We must remind ourselves that there are virtually no smooth novel forms of the kind that Moretti and Jameson imagine migrating haplessly to premodern social realities, traveling to people who have only content and no form producing the "awkward" novel of the nonmodern West. Intrusive narrators, unlikely plots, and historical characters show up in all nineteenth-century fiction. "Formalism," as William Ghosh has pointed out, "registers as much a 'desire for form' as an identification or analysis thereof."[19]

Curiously, we have taken Moretti's word on a host of national literatures that he "reads" through critics: it's very hard to find any "fact-checking" of his readings. After an intensive engagement with the bibliography of "Conjectures on World Literature," it is difficult for me to see any "law" develop, let alone the one that underwrites Jameson's formal travel ban. Some critics do seem to prove Jameson's "awkward" theory. Masao Miyoshi, for example, in discussing Ōgai's novel *The Wild Goose*, writes that "The narrative structure . . . is a bit awkward, a frequent problem with Japanese novels. The narrator, Okada's friend, begins by reminiscing on past events, but soon disappears from the tale, almost making it a third-person story. He returns in chapter 18 when it becomes increasingly clumsy to present events which the narrator cannot have been in a position to know."[20] This is very much like the narrative structure of *Madame Bovary*, which starts with a first-person narrator who then disappears until the end of the novel. *Madame Bovary* isn't, to my knowledge, described by critics as awkward.[21] Indeed, the brokenness

19. William Ghosh, "The Formalist Genesis of 'Postcolonial' Reading: Brathwaite, Bhabha, and *A House for Mr. Biswas*," ELH 84, no. 3 (2017): 765.

20. Masao Miyoshi, *Accomplices of Silence: The Modern Japanese Novel* (Berkeley: University of California Press, 1974), 48; qtd. in J. Keith Vincent, *Two-Timing Modernity: Homosocial Narrative in Modern Japanese Fiction* (Cambridge, MA: Harvard University Press, 2012), 56.

21. A notable exception is Kent Puckett, *Bad Form: Social Mistakes and the*

of its form does not receive much in the way of comment, since Flaubert is the ur-objective novelist.

If we read the critical studies Moretti cites, they not only don't all corroborate his generalization of Jameson's observation, but the ideas of numerous critics are also distorted or quoted in a way that garbles the larger argument: we find, for example, that Schwarz is after something more profound than an argument about "half-baked" nineteenth-century Brazilian novels. He argues that in the case of the Brazilian novelist (and jurist) José de Alencar, for example, realist fiction "is inconsistent at its core; but its inconsistency merely repeats in a purified and developed form the essential dilemma of our ideological position in Brazil, and is its effect and restatement."[22] This seems to me to be an excellent description of the "Western" form of the novel as adumbrated by Jameson himself in *The Political Unconscious*: fiction gives us an inconsistency to consider the difference between what we have and what we want, between historical actuality and a dream of its repair.

Ato Quayson, rather than capitulate to the stereotype of the singularity of the premodern orality of the Nigerian (and "African") story-telling tradition, points out that all literacy and therefore literature depend on orality, "the possibility of oralization": "[t]his is because processes of verbal recall, either in the form of paraphrasing, summarizing, rephrasing or oral commentary are a valued part of any literate culture."[23] Quayson proposes the valuable concept of "interdiscursivity" to understand African literature, and it seems to me a concept that moves quite well beyond that continent.[24] Our sense of any text is always

---

Nineteenth-Century Novel (Oxford: Oxford University Press, 2008). See especially chapter 2, "Embarrasing *Bovary*," 53–82.

22. Roberto Schwarz and John Gledson, *Misplaced Ideas: Essays on Brazilian Culture* (London: Verso, 1992), 63.

23. Ato Quayson, *Strategic Transformations in Nigerian Writing: Orality and History in the Work of Reverend Samuel Johnson, Amos Tutuola, Wole Soyinka, and Ben Okri* (Bloomington: Indiana University Press, 1997), 14.

24. Ibid., 17, 121.

informed by the nontextual, or by discourses that may be far removed from the literary, as New Historicist and other kinds of contextualizing criticisms have suggested. There is nothing that I can find in *Strategic Transformations in Nigerian Literature* that supports Moretti's argument, or Jameson's "law."

Moretti pounces with particular delight on Henry Zhao's work on late Qing fiction, tellingly titled "The Uneasy Narrator." This title underscores the idea that Chinese narrators are awkward in their formal role: "A salient feature of late Qing fiction is the greater frequency of narrative intrusions than in any previous period of Chinese vernacular fiction."[25] The subtlety of Zhao's argument is lost here: his point is that "with some generalization, we can say that the narrator in traditional Chinese fiction is . . . comfortably domineering."[26] In late Qing fiction this situation changes, and narrators become "confident in organizing a rebellion in the narrated world against the fiction-producing world." This seems to me to be characteristic of various strains not only of modernist writing, but also of realism. Wendy Veronica Xin has argued that from Jane Austen to Hitchcock, there are characters who function as "plotters," who, like Zhao's narrator, make trouble between story and discourse—indeed, the "space" between these narrative levels is a place for social climbing and social change: "that literary character whose schemes and conspiracies rouse the novel's 'narratable' material into being and who becomes strangely entangled with both narrative content and narrative form."[27] But perhaps the most relevant thing to point out about Zhao's argument is that he is not discussing Chinese fiction and Flaubert; he is writing about the history of Chinese fiction without much reference to the mighty West.

25. Henry Y. H. Zhao, *The Uneasy Narrator: Chinese Fiction from the Traditional to the Modern* (New York: Oxford University Press, 1995); qtd. in Moretti, "Conjectures on World Literature," 63n24.

26. Zhao, *The Uneasy Narrator*, 4.

27. Wendy Veronica Xin, "The Importance of Being Frank," *NOVEL: A Forum on Fiction* 52, no. 1 (May 2019): 23–43.

Kōjin Karatani, in *Origins of Modern Japanese Literature*, questions the solidity of the "nineteenth-century Western novel" as an interpretive matrix. He attributes to the theorist and novelist Sōseki a "positive will" attached to Sōseki's inability or refusal "to accommodate the modern novel."[28] Karatani also denies the "maturation" process that Sōseki has often been praised for: he has often been seen by critics as moving from the unrealistic toward the realistic, in a trajectory the "peripheral" novelist must always seem to follow.[29] Instead, Karatani argues that Sōseki, like Flaubert, wrote in a myriad of genres, and that perhaps the novel is nothing so much as the extinction of genre itself.

Meenakshi Mukherjee, whom Moretti presents as taking an almost pitying stance toward Indian attempts at realism, is in fact highly critical of the realism Indian writers relied on: "It is perhaps unfortunate that the nineteenth-century Indian novelist had as his model primarily the British Victorian novel."[30] She regrets that "India's first generation of novelists had hardly any access to Tolstoy, Melville or Flaubert."[31] The idea of "Western form" is absent from Mukherjee's analysis: she thinks instead about the variety of national novel forms, and how much Indian writers might have benefitted from a literary decolonization.

Indeed, the idea that "Western" makes sense as a naturalized adjective (a reference to a place or region) has been effectively cancelled by the work of Saree Makdisi, who documents the slow growth and adaptation in nineteenth-century England of "Western" as an idea and a descriptor. Throughout the eighteenth century, both the poor and the aristocracy were described in Orientalist terms, Makdisi claims, accused of "indulgence,

28. Kōjin Karatani, *Origins of Modern Japanese Literature*, trans. Brett de Bary (Durham, NC: Duke University Press, 1993), 176.

29. Ibid., 175.

30. Meenakshi Mukherjee, *Realism and Reality: The Novel and Society in India* (Oxford: Oxford University Press, 1996), 27.

31. Ibid., 17–18.

passion, rage, an embarrassing lack of self-control, etc."[32] Locating the Occident and determining (inventing) the characteristics of the Western subject was a monumental struggle, involving a host of cultural players, including poets, economists, and philosophers. A massive interdisciplinary labor was required to invent a "world of individual, self-regulating subjects priding themselves on their moral virtues [who] would necessarily control Others who were not seen as equally moral or capable of self-regulation."[33] The "Western" form of the novel is a similar artifact: a model that non-Western people can't get quite right. Of course the assumption, belied by a number of the non-"Western" scholars cited above, is that the whole world longs to write in a form that may be a chimera. As Edoard Glissant has it, "The West is not in the West. It is a project not a place."[34]

The novel may not have a formal history at all; instead, it might have a history of readings that have created a rich set of what might be seen, from a certain point of view, as unlikely assemblages: centuries or half-centuries in which punctual formal changes arrive, or changes that arrive with the reigns of monarchs or the between times of wars. More such assemblages might be tried out in the service of reading more novels outside of an assigned historical regimen of development that will always leave some people and places struggling to catch up in a story of literary history that might itself be a fiction, and a deeply pernicious one at that: it controls not only our curricula but our residual ideas about civilizations and cultures—ideas that should be left behind while we allow "peripheral" literatures and the neglected wisdom of their critics to come more fully into view when we think about what novels do. Questions about the

32. Saree Makdisi, *Making England Western: Occidentalism, Race, and Imperial Culture* (Chicago: University of Chicago Press, 2013), 17.

33. Ibid., 241.

34. Edoard Glissant, "Introductions," in *Caribbean Discourse: Selected Essays*, trans. J. Michael Dash (Charlottesville: University of Virginia Press, 1989), 2n1.

very finely adumbrated study of British Literature might be usefully asked after considering our critical fictions, and our curricula might change accordingly.

The "muddled" narrator of Laurent Binet's novel *HhHH* "want[s] to believe that people exist even if we don't speak of them."[35] Of course they do, and their novels exist too, but not for those of us who do not speak of them as part of a history of the novel, a history of culture, a history of the world that we have chosen to speak of as if we know the very particular little bit of it that matters.

35. Lauren Binet, *HHhH: A Novel* (New York: Picador, 2013), 323.

INDEX

A NOTE ON THE TYPE

{~~~~~~~~~~}

THIS BOOK has been composed in Miller, a Scotch Roman typeface designed by Matthew Carter and first released by Font Bureau in 1997. It resembles Monticello, the typeface developed for The Papers of Thomas Jefferson in the 1940s by C. H. Griffith and P. J. Conkwright and reinterpreted in digital form by Carter in 2003.

Pleasant Jefferson ("P. J.") Conkwright (1905–1986) was Typographer at Princeton University Press from 1939 to 1970. He was an acclaimed book designer and AIGA Medalist.

The ornament used throughout this book was designed by Pierre Simon Fournier (1712–1768) and was a favorite of Conkwright's, used in his design of the *Princeton University Library Chronicle*.